Furious

'A passionate guidebook to feminist theorising that refuses data as self-evident patterns and theory as beautiful abstractions, while insisting on the generative power of writing, fabulation, and future making.'

Lucy Suchman, author of *Feminist STS and the Sciences of the Artificial*

'This wide-ranging and imaginative book makes a compelling case for a feminist techno-politics which challenges to the core the masculinist grip of computational culture and science. It's also a book which pays fine attention to the process of writing.'

Angela McRobbie, author of *Be Creative: Making a Living in the New Culture Industries*

Digital Barricades:
Interventions in Digital Culture and Politics

Series editors:
Professor Jodi Dean, Hobart and William Smith Colleges
Dr Joss Hands, Newcastle University
Professor Tim Jordan, University of Sussex

Also available:

Shooting a Revolution:
Visual Media and Warfare in Syria
Donatella Della Ratta

Inhuman Power:
Artificial Intelligence and the Future of Capitalism
Nick Dyer-Witheford, Atle Mikkola Kjosen and James Steinhoff

Cyber-Proletariat:
Global Labour in the Digital Vortex
Nick Dyer-Witheford

The Digital Party:
Political Organisation and Online Democracy
Paolo Gerbaudo

Gadget Consciousness:
Collective Thought, Will and Action in the Age of Social Media
Joss Hands

Information Politics:
Liberation and Exploitation in the Digital Society
Tim Jordan

Sad by Design:
On Platform Nihilism
Geert Lovink

Unreal Objects:
Digital Materialities, Technoscientific Projects and Political Realities
Kate O'Riordan

Furious

Technological Feminism and Digital Futures

Caroline Bassett, Sarah Kember, Kate O'Riordan

PLUTO  PRESS

First published 2020 by Pluto Press
345 Archway Road, London N6 5AA

www.plutobooks.com

British Library Cataloguing in Publication Data
A catalogue record for this book is available from the British Library

ISBN   978 0 7453 4049 4   Hardback
ISBN   978 0 7453 4050 0   Paperback
ISBN   978 1 7868 0565 2   PDF eBook
ISBN   978 1 7868 0567 6   Kindle eBook
ISBN   978 1 7868 0566 9   EPUB eBook

Typeset by Stanford DTP Services, Northampton, England

Simultaneously printed in the United Kingdom and United States of America

For our mothers

Contents

Series Preface

Crisis and conflict open up opportunities for liberation. In the early twenty-first century, these moments are marked by struggles enacted over and across the boundaries of the virtual, the digital, the actual, and the real. Digital cultures and politics connect people even as they simultaneously place them under surveillance and allow their lives to be mined for advertising. This series aims to intervene in such cultural and political conjunctures. It features critical explorations of the new terrains and practices of resistance, producing critical and informed explorations of the possibilities for revolt and liberation.

Emerging research on digital cultures and politics investigates the effects of the widespread digitization of increasing numbers of cultural objects, the new channels of communication swirling around us and the changing means of producing, remixing and distributing digital objects. This research tends to oscillate between agendas of hope, that make remarkable claims for increased participation, and agendas of fear, that assume expanded repression and commodification. To avoid the opposites of hope and fear, the books in this series aggregate around the idea of the barricade. As sources of enclosure as well as defenses for liberated space, barricades are erected where struggles are fierce and the stakes are high. They are necessarily partisan divides, different politicizations and deployments of a common surface. In this sense, new media objects, their networked circuits and settings, as well as their material, informational, and biological carriers all act as digital barricades.

Jodi Dean, Joss Hands and Tim Jordan

Acknowledgements

We wrote this over a longer time than we intended. The benefit of this was that we had extended conversations with many more people – face-to-face, virtually, at our respective institutions and far beyond. We'd especially like to acknowledge the Helsinki Collegium for Advanced Studies, and the Sussex Humanities Lab, both of which hosted writing sessions, and in the case of the Lab, public presentations. Susanna Paasonen read an early draft and cooked us dinner – thanks for both. Joan Haran was also an excellent reader. Thank you very much to our anonymous readers and reviewers whose feedback helped us understand the nature of the intervention we made. Specific thanks to Maggie Williams for telling us about the Brockengespenst phenomenon.

Preface

Furious: Technological Feminism and Digital Futures is an angry feminist intervention disputing the masculinization of computational culture and cultural theory. It draws on feminist genealogies, traditions of writing and approaches to science and technology in order to provide an alternative to heavily material and object oriented turns and to the masculinism, scientism and anti-feminism that dominate both cultural and knowledge production.

The book highlights the need to contest the regressively gendered and very often sexist politics of digital media forms, practices and study. It stresses the need to counter ideologies of scientism and anti-feminism and to reconnect feminist practices of thinking and writing with the contemporary problematic in order to re-conceptualize digital media and broader technological futures, pervasive mediation and increasing automation.

Technological transformations are accelerating in the world. There is a tendency in digital technology and innovation to celebrate the new, to rely on the technical fix and to promise futures in which good consumers are empowered. Discourses of big data dominate in political, economic and educational fields as well as in practices of media consumption. At the same time, the fields of digital media and digital humanities scholarship have a tendency to venerate technical forms and essences and to adopt gendered writing and citation practices. This is marked by, for example, the way that critical theory is considered separate from feminist thought, and the way that the material turn, object orientation and scientism is valourized. In this context, it is important to intervene, to offer a critique, and to contest those writing practices and politics. This book does so by foregrounding feminist traditions and contributions to media and cultural theory. Its aim is to offer alternative modes of knowledge production and to outline intersectional feminist values and visions of digital media and technological futures. *Furious: Technological Feminism and Digital Futures* frames the digital as a space of antagonism within which it is possible to rethink critical and political positions, including feminism. It does so in order to reformulate a sense of where we are, as differentiated subjects in techno-culture, and to rethink what needs to be done.

The book operationalizes its critique through structure and writing styles as well as scholarship. This preface provides a guide into the mode of address adopted in the introductory chapter, which is followed by three inquiries and a conclusion. The first chapter intervenes in the field through a mode of feminist poetics drawn from a history of collaborations and forms of address within feminist writing. The three inquiry chapters which follow do their work through an attention to: 1) bodies and selves; 2) work and home; and 3) environment and world. The final chapter develops a set of propositions about futures, knowledge and technology. The text draws attention to questions of authorship and citation, and stresses the validity of the modes of writing explored in the inquiry chapters.

Co-written by three leading scholars in the field of feminist media and science and technology studies, this book generates a playful, serious, writerly and furious tradition of feminist critique, in order to challenge the erasure of feminism and the (attendant) gendering of technological environments in the present, and in order to contest the technocratic utopias that are too often aligned with media theory and masculine metaphysics.

The book's introduction is interventional in form and content. It is a form of poetic writing that recalls a specific tradition of feminist writing and that signals, thereby, an incursion into the current problematic, understood as the digital, or post-digital. Here, the authors outline a concern with the naturalization of the digital: of big data, smart things and computable everything. They identify a collusion in this respect, between industry and academia, and argue that too often media theorizing and technological fantasizing come together in the pursuit of beautiful abstractions – of unmediated things in themselves. Asking the rhetorical question of who needs language in a subjectless, extinct, object oriented world, this chapter maintains that absenting ourselves, as humans (albeit as humans in differential relations with technology) from our own futures, engaging in fantasies in which an automated world inscribes itself, is a dangerous sleight of hand, a trick that feminist writing, that feminists writing together, might yet undo.

'Scale, Subject and Stories: Unreal Objects' examines the genome as a beautiful abstraction and a mode of technological fantasizing that scales up from one to many, the individual genome to the population and the species, promising future lives of preservation and post-human perfection. By rescaling to the story of one particular subject, 'my mother', this chapter demonstrates how the fantasy of the genome as a thing in itself, an unreal object inscribing the future of life, is precisely a dangerous sleight of hand, a fatal trick played on one life, a fable that this instance of feminist writing can reveal and re-story, but in this case, not undo.

'Bland Ambition? Automation's Missing Visions' revisits concepts of freedom and control, technological reduction and augmentation at a time when the automation of home and domestic work is once again accelerating, reproducing a nostalgically gendered narrative and iconography that demands feminist inquiry and intervention. It begins with a critique of automation fever – speculations about the end of work, for example – as both narrow in focus and lacking ambition, failing to see beyond gendered divisions of home and work, leisure and labour, production and reproduction. If automation fever (incorporating many current theories of accelerationism) offers familiar, linear, smooth and predictable passageways to the future, in which gender and social division no longer seem to matter, what alternate or missing visions might feminism offer? What more ambitious future might we imagine and what role does automation play in it?

'Driving At The Anthropocene, or, Let's Get Out of Here: How?' calls for an end to the circular, endgame scenarios of the Anthropocene, in which the survival of technological man ('there never was a technological woman') – of Man and his tools – is predicated on his extinction. It uses driving as a narratological device for thinking (driving at) and moving through the world differently, in between divisions of salvation and damnation, ends and beginnings; the rocks and hard places that trap some subjects more than others, precluding their mutual becoming in, and with the environment. Such entrapment, understood here as the futility and false universality of the 'we're [all] fucked' version of the Anthropocene, recalls the Jewish, French Algerian, Feminist theorist Hélène Cixous' 1970s injunction: 'let's get out of here!' The pertinent question, one that the chapter goes on to explore, is 'how?' In doing so, it identifies the need to transit from one protagonist's point of view to those it excludes.

The final chapter is part summary and part projection. Following the previous chapter, which seeks to decolonize the debate on future environments by driving out of the anthroposcene, it outlines a concept of radical intersectionality as a modus operandi, a way of living better together with, through and as technology (at all scales).

It also offers a performance review with a difference: a review of the book's performances. What were we trying, not only to say, but to *do*, in our writing? How far did we get? How to go on? Perhaps from manifesto to manual – in an attempt to avoid reproducing the same old politics, divisions of thought and compensatory habits of mind, this chapter sets out a series of propositions for radically intersectional feminist techno-futures, propositions that might contribute to a manual, or indicate how to move towards a future that is rescaled, re-storied, more ambitious and more just.

1
Feminist Futures: A Conditional Paeon for the Anything-Digital

paeon
n. (in classical prosody) a foot of one long and three short syllables in any order

(thefreedictionary.com)

paean, paeon, peon
A paean (pronounced PEE-in, sometimes spelled pean) is a fervent expression of joy or praise, often in song.

A paeon (pronounced PEE-in or PEE-on) is a four-syllable metrical foot in prosody. Anyone who doesn't analyze poetry will never have a use for the word.

A peon (pronounced PEE-on) is an unskilled laborer or menial worker. Today, use of the word is most common in Indian English, where it's used to describe any worker and presumably doesn't have negative connotations. In American and British English, peon has an insulting tone. No one, in the US at least, wants to be a peon.

The first two words have origins in the same Greek term; peon comes from the Medieval Latin term for foot soldier.

(grammarist.com)

This is a metrical book in one long and, in any order, three shorter chapters: a four-syllable metrical foot in prosody. Thus, a paeon, of a kind, about the digital or post-digital; we don't care which. One is shorthand for a formation it does not describe. The second labels a change within that formation we do not necessarily accept. This is a form of poetic writing that wants to grapple with our contemporary constellation. This is not a book about labels.

This constellation, from our point of view, orbits around the attractions of big data, of computable everything, of smart things, of clean diagrams, beautiful patterns, future environments: of worlds that are made into data and then into something else. New cleaner, smarter, more real versions of life, which just is, which denies the crafting that goes into making it look like that. It gravitates towards an architecture that aims for ubiquity, invisibility and control, while making a world of devices, applications and algorithms.

The current constellation configures a technocratic world of endless new media, although it doesn't need to take that shape. At the same time, some of those that might contest it have given up the tools that would enable them to intervene. Media theorizing and technological fantasizing too often come together in the pursuit of beautiful abstractions. Big data patterns media theory as much as it does the politics of technology. Machine logics, data analytics and the archaeologies of media-in-themselves (dug out of what, by who, to what end?) are the new languages of media. They have emerged because of an apparent consensus that we are all – and equally – post-human now. Who needs language in a subjectless, extinct, anthropocenic (not anthropocentric?) object oriented world? Wherever do subjects and stories go in worlds of wonderful, world-changing technological things? In a world of code, who writes about the end of writing? Absenting ourselves from our futures is a sleight of hand. 'We' humans re-enter the scene unseen, a specter: the subject that haunts the object. Are we dealing once again with archetypes?

As the archetypal subject re-presents itself in its absence and in the declaration of its ending at the hands of the digital, it is important, once again, once upon this time, to relate to our differences. There is no universal, no absolute, no end, no beginning, no ontological distinctions and substitutions. 'We' continue to coexist differently in, and differentially as the world of dynamic matter, lively computers, and mediation. Now to that other 'we'; as writers, as the authors of this book, we three are quite happy with translations and transformations: data, text, body – when they are recognized as circular, multiply directed, iterative and not closed. What we want to refuse, as well as the most simplistic of substitutions, subjects for objects, humans for things, is a particular series of declensions: roughly those that turn bodies to text, texts to data, data to diagrams, and that then purge this final figure, the diagram, the architecture, of its impure pasts. These are the dominant modes of the computational, big data and materialism. But to say this again: this mode – body, text, data, diagram – there's nothing wrong with this. The problem comes when what comes at the end, the diagram, the beautiful structure, the new machine, refuses to accept or acknowledge where it came from, and gives itself as the only possible answer, *the* solution. Dissolving into itself its component parts it re-renders itself as beyond all that old fashioning: creating beautiful abstractions.

It might be useful to note that this declension itself gets reduced still further: text and data. No bodies at all, never mind subjects. And no need to think about the complexity of the diagram, only to see it as data speaking itself and thereby speaking its irreducible truth. Information is beautiful. Information in, data out. We maintain that this – though it had a moment with the text – is not writing.

Declension produces a story that lively materials generate information and data, and are fully understandable in those forms. For example, genomes are sequenced and made as data, patterning new versions of life-like engineered organisms, printed as a book of life that tells no story, but just is. Or lives are cleaned up and cut up through the forms that take to data; photos, comments, likes and shares. Big biomedia and small social media both make a world known through forms in which information science, big data architects, search and algorithms become the necessary way of knowing. That's the story given about computation, big data and the solutions it provides. This is a story that refuses to call itself a story; that says story doesn't count. And it isn't an accident that this suddenly looks like that savage reduction of narrative itself to the binary: in/out. Narrative into sadism; we must either *be* seduced by beautiful information, or *consent* to be seduced by it. It is a narratological violence that has its connections to older links between formalism, cybernetics, and structuralism. Interpretation, meaning, alternative desires and whole lives are cut out of a story that explains itself in its own terms while denying its own storytelling capacities.

Of course they tell a good story, those chief architects of life after new media, those corporate voices that sometimes seem to be humans (the Founders, the Entrepreneurs, the Architects, all of them puissant only because of their industrial extensions). They use all the tools in the book to do it, including eliding realism with the coming real: blueprints, future visions and prototypes. Their scientifically designed futures are science fictions, we should recall, and like other science fictions, they exploit all forms of the possible real, to produce an affective engagement with the tale. You'd better believe it, because this is really coming!

Too many of the demigods of object oriented media theory tell these kinds of stories too. They also deny that they are telling tales, even while their storytelling is all too apparent. Look at their fantastic construction of desirable worlds made of gadgets and impossible anatomies, mountains that speak, objects that hum, people in the right order, a leveled out space in which objects give us new forms of enlightenment, to which we freely attend, and entrance to which is freely given – 'women are welcome here' – they say. These though are tributary tales; the mainstream comes from the fable makers of the computational industries.

Computational industries give us fables of an inevitable time to come. They give us a post-political conflict-free epic, a myth of benign digital conquest, that scales all ways: from the newly made heroes of the deep history of computing, geological forms, renaissance artists; to the founders of the valley; all the way up from invisible information infra-structures; the beneath and beyond perceptible logics of algorithm and database; to autonomous modes of transport, smart-glass homes and cities and global – if not cosmic – connectivity.

The world that these founders made, their imaginary universe, or the universe of their hubris, potently performative, is multi-scalar and highly structured. It is resigned to inequality – although also politely regrets it – while actively redesigning it. It serves everyone everywhere (though some a lot more than others), and is centered on neutralized, un-differentiated data-connected, muted (we have voice recognition technologies for that old speaking and writing routine), object-filtered, always already enhanced and optimized, declined, substituted, techno-subjects. Citizen tech is a universal figure, indifferent to difference, carved out of its own self-same consumer category, a seamless match, a perfect pairing; the very manifestation of its object correlative. We have Janet for her smart kitchen and John for his kitted out car. The universal segues, in all manner of tech driven visions, narratives, promotions, into the opti-mized, perfected and above all productive citizen of our times. Indeed what is being driven at here is universal productivity, the generating if not working citizen; we're heading in a different direction.

It is tempting to hate this world, and its totalitarian way of dealing with its gendered techno-subjects, but here comes the trickiness: it wraps servitude in a promise of personal service, and is in this way seductive. Everybody is special. There are no ugly sisters, but only those, 7.53 billion to whom proper attention is paid. They are served in order to be served up as data. Technology humbles itself in order to be crowned through translations, declensions and substitutions. We are back to weird tales and fairy stories.

Let's twist their tales and write our own.

And, since we've invoked the ugly sisters, let's begin with glass slippers and Cinderella subjects. Let's talk of the magical properties of manufactured glass, a mirror for the modern myths of the anything-digital world. In this new world, Cinderella subjects, scullery maids for nuclear families, Cinderella-everybodies, are immediately recognized as the rightful heirs to glass slippers, dodging the unproductive ugly sisters, who are pacified by their own magical mirrors.

Cinderella's new slipper is a speech-enabled translucent kitchen worktop that asks her if she'd like help with her baking, or an augmented reality bathroom mirror that displays a punishing schedule of meetings before she has brushed her teeth.

Cinderella's new slipper is a transparent interactive screen that obliges her to programme the home ambient intelligence system while checking her to-do list and getting children off to school. It is her car windscreen that counts down the time to her destination in seconds and the ubiquitous default health app on her phone through which she must measure her steps, calories, sleep, contacts, likes, loves and life.

Cinderella is both potential and *potentia*. She does not get to choose which. Her time is cut out for her, cut in to her, carved up into an increasingly unsustainable, fine-grained pattern of work-rest-and-play. She is reconstituted and re-ordered in time even as she continues to emerge *as time* (as life itself). She is the menial, domestic and professional worker without end – a real peon: a real labourer for the post-digital.

In this new world, you don't want to be Cinderella, yet she is everywhere, luminously reflected, projected, magnified and rotated in twenty-first century glass worlds. As for the others – the ugly sisters have had their faces smoothed, their ungovernable tempers tempered, and their smiles painted on; they're fit for the labour of social media and are busy posting to Instagram. So how are they different now, from Cinderella? And the scullery maids? They have been automated out of existence – fully redundant figures in the new economy.

This everybody-Cinderella, the heroine of the old tales like it or not (perhaps she always hated the prince), is now the figure for a new sexual contract. Cinderella is a constitutive part of a transparent environment that is intuitive, affective, gestural, sensory and haptic. She can speak or be seen; voice or visibility, not both. She unlearns to write, courtesy of predictive texts and voice-recognition software that promises to say it all for her. Automation re-organizes the shift from voice to written inscription, threatening to take away that moment of making distance between speaking and writing, between what is captured and what is thought. Retain the breath, but close the distance.

This is the future that has, for a long time, been in design. It was the future of the 1950s when the correlation of technics and life was distilled into times and spaces for the containment and proliferation of female labour, and into new regimes and techniques of productivity and reproductivity in an era of Cold War. Now Microsoft, no less than Monsanto, puts Cinderella back in the kitchen. The difference is that in the 50s, Monsanto's kitchen was made of melamine. Now Microsoft's (Google's, Corning's) kitchen is made of glass. Glass is the new plastic. Glass is the new skin, the sensual, thin, flexible, soon-to-be elastic (post-plastic) material that wraps around Cinderella's body, first transforming it, then transforming *into* it, a proper grotesque, a grimmer fairy tale future.

The architects of today's infrastructure are part of the same economy as the smaller games and wearable technology industries. For instance, those who design 'chastity' bras that pop open when our prince comes and those who make violently misogynistic games and then react with violent misogyny when they are challenged for doing so. Under the conditions of impossibility of the new sexual contract, voice or visibility, labour or life, what is to be done?

Let's twist again: Cinderella could do something else. As writers, we can direct our characters, set them on a different path, or place them in a different universe, real or imagined. Which might be the point; our Cinderella stays with mediation. Nothing appears to her without being made communicable. A new or old world is not conjured directly from atoms, or quarks, or geology, or imagination without processes of communication, pictures, language, forms, connections, negotiations. She does not conspire with the nowhere and everywhere point of view, nor turn away from the cultural and textual.

Everything is full of meaning, but who is to say what and how that meaning is made. After all, in the fairy tale, Cinderella's mice were horses, and vegetables were her carriage. That was magic. But in this scientific, or rather scientist world, it is also the case that anything can be something else (pig fuckers become prime ministers, gropers become presidents, etc). The point is that *whose* something gets to count as the real thing, is up for grabs. Meaning was never perfect, meaning and mattering always slip and slide, you have to grab onto something. The question is, what? Neurology, materialisms and other ontologically oriented approaches look for what's solid. Absolutist medium theory alights on the technology as the message and evacuates the content. How then can the world appear? Cinderella eschews such purifications and knows that pages and pictures, symbols and texts, count as part of the world too; are in fact intrinsic to it.

Writing counts.

So does writing new stories. And we begin by saying that these things we are given as uncontestable coming realities, inevitable developments, *are* stories. If this book itself is also story (which it is), it is a different one. It is one that contests the demands of technological stories to become mythical prediction. We reject their attempt to act as performative origin stories, forms of future prediction that set out to *make* what they say will come, a snapped shut circle.

We want to find different accounts, and new possibilities, and we look around, therefore, for other allies. Those who see literary forms as material things that provoke actions but are not executable. Those with critical views of technology too, and those who claim interventional expertise, doubled, redoubled, tripled, intelligences, those who know they can make a difference.

All too often though, what we find when we look for allies, are the old princes, naked and ornate, who know there are some problems with this looking glass world, but are – let's face it – easily enchanted. And who would want to give away the role of the prince, with its illusion of action, for the life of the princess, bound into the tale, as she is foot-bound by her glass shoes?

These princes, particularly the ones *who choose* to be princes, the demigods of particular kinds of theory, are complicit in this future. Some evoke figures of furious women in the service of producing entirely man-made theories of everything and forgetting about bodies, abandoning identities. They see everything from nowhere, at one with the world of things that just are, or very soon will be. They ask what it is like to be glass, sliding in to become transparent, using this as justification for their failure to take a standpoint of their own. They do not ask what this glass does, how it makes a cut, who bleeds. They are willfully ignorant of Cinderella's eye view and don't, in any case, think it matters.

They have abandoned any interest in those divisions between service/ servitude, flattened out affect and texture, smoothed over divisions that organize humans, and are far more interested in other forms of empathy:

how to feel like code, how glass moves, and at what fascinating, scintillating scales. Absolute speed and molecular sloth.

They think we are all 'after humanity' and thereby think it's fine to ignore, or simply refuse to reveal, the mess that Cinderella is in. The particular grotesque of skin and glass, glass as skin – the transparent morphing in, and as time, disciplined by service/servitude, that constitutes her day's labour. And remember that Cinderella is the figure for ourselves, the digital subjects.

These theoretical demigods believe, with the architects (as the architects) in the *potentia* of glass. They affirm and attest this *potentia*, having no more need for the negativity of critique.

As part of that, they have relinquished language – or so they say. Narratives do not matter; representation is always false. Matter is all that matters. Matter is all that matters. Matter is all that matters. This is a chant. This is a paean for the post-digital. And hearing it, Cinderellas everywhere (also everyware and everywear), and those are who in danger of *becoming* Cinderellas, should beware. You are the peon the paean is not sung for. Your future is to be cut out. Or be cut in. Either way you serve, and are served up, and badly served, denied the tools to speak and write – even while forced to become productive.

But like we said, let's twist again.

Suppose you refuse to be *that* Cinderella? Suppose the tail/tale didn't wag for you, that you didn't wear it; the whiteness, heteronormativity, class aspiration, universal subjectivity, even as myth? Well, then, or so you were told, you could try out at being the prince (but even then . . .). Beyond those two roles, they warned, was only the abyss of the unnamed, bit characters, plot functions without function, actants without agency (human or machine), illegitimacy and indeterminacy.

Those divisions don't work, at least if you think freedom matters. There are places and bodies in between. We want to jump into the abyss. From there we can rethink what bodies are, and what subjects are, and what biotechnological subjects might become – and what a new politics of the material might be.

We refuse to be saved like Cinderella, we don't want to be saved; it should be obvious why. It's been clear, at least since Microsoft Word, and certainly since *The Circle*, that salvation is a form of capture. That's precisely why – as Margaret Atwood noted, its Cinderella heroine is herself a distress signal – Mae Day; May Day, M'aidez; help me, MeToo. This might become a call for some solidarity.

Another kind of other salvage operation, our own, begins by refusing the tale that refuses the tale, as the start of its own tale. So here are the bare bones of a different story.

This is a story of whatever and wherever digital media, and of whatever, wherever, whoever. It is about the fabulated composite writing body we constitute, and it looks for differently constituted bodies than our own. We are an agglomeration, an intersection; we make no claims at all to be complete.

Although our fabulation still turns on Cinderella's swollen feet, our inelegant pirouette can turn at different scales, and has greater ambitions to intersect. We're not giving scale, subjectivity or new forms of collectivity away to the mountain viewers.

PAEAN, PAEON, PEONS AND WRITING

So here it is. Our four-syllable paeon – a metrical book in one long and, in any order, three short chapters (who's counting?). Impure poetry, you might say. We do. Which is not to say we are poets. We'd rather name ourselves peons. Peons: menial labourers. How can we include ourselves in this category given our professor-ated natures, and good jobs, our white western status? Incredulity might seem a reasonable response. Bear with us. We have our reasons.

The first: we are peons because we work on texts, labour on them, by hand, by highly augmented, automated hand. We have no problem with automation *per se*; dividing bodies and machines was last century's debate. It's not where we draw lines now, and was an old red line we never respected anyway. How could anybody who read Haraway seriously? And we did.

So no red lines. But instead: inscription ensembles involving keyboards and screens, keys and pages, pens and paper, hands and heads. Writing. We are peons because we are enamoured of the labour of writing. We want to recognize that by-handedness, that particular labour that is supposedly to be automated out of existence, but that continues to inform, inscribe, be inscripted into contemporary computational formations. We are enamoured not least because the labour of writing is systemically devalued in that recent tradition of the digital which denies its own form, preferring formations from which all that is not absolutely inhuman is to be expunged (ideally), or regarded as only an obstacle to getting to the real, not the real event but the pure essence, the quiddity of the thing.

Second, we enroll ourselves as peons because we claim solidarity with others. We write with an awareness that many of these others have lives far, far harder than our own. But we are – like almost everybody else – increasingly made peon-ic by neoliberalism, in our case through our interpellation into the academy with its flexible, extensible, wrap-around desires to own us. And its assumption that it always has the right to demand more, or to spit us out if our label no longer fits whatever re-fit, whichever revamp or newly metrical measure is provided (back to paeons too then; it's our metrical measures against those valourized in the academy).

Finally, we are peons because we are women. Because we are feminists, and because we are feminist women writing about the digital. Because we declare that there is work to be done, and that it demands peons to do it. Because we are casting a vote of no confidence in the emergent politicians of post-human, post-digital environments and networked, distributed, intelligent things-in-themselves. Specifically, we do not care what it is like to be a computer, or not when this query enacts a fantasy of unmediation; of things that just are, and of human-technological futures that write themselves. That world view has no room for questions concerning solidarity, equality, or – let us invoke a word that is almost quaint these days – liberation; meaning this to frame demands for freedom that go far beyond simple equality (although they begin with it), because they are also demands to reopen horizons, to begin to imagine and develop radical transformations.

This is where we stand in relation to the labour of writing. We defend this labour and seek to augment it as far as possible. This is not an anti-computing thesis. Writing is central to us. And we see our labour *as* a labour in writing. Labouring to inscribe and to accept the distance between writing and voice, to have both. We are writing to speak. Amongst other things.

This means we are working with writing tools. We won't give them away, not least because we have noticed that the nominal, anonymised, normative, he-who-shall-not-be-named media theorist, who may think he is amongst the demigods, declares he is willing to relinquish, (or rather, be seen to relinquish) tools at his disposal – including narrative, poetry, storytelling, representation and critique. Meanwhile, the architects of the post-digital universe – those residing currently at Google (*et. al.*) are emphatically not.

Our work is to engage with the gendered politics of an increasingly computationally infused life after new media, by which we mean all of the technology and all of the life (everyday life, environmental life, the half life of robots, our own vital life). A work by hand, but also a work deploying all the tools that make us, and that remain, even if contingently, at our disposal. Writing may be with or in code. The difference is, that as such it still recognises that meaning as well as computation informs what is written. We see this as labour that is menial, once meaning: of the household. It is menial because it refuses particular flights of fantasy or particular kinds of grandiosity and because it is both automated and done by hand. It does not rely wholly on automation and automation's self-referentiality.

As feminists, as critics of unreflective forms of the deification of the material, we claim a political subjectivity that is necessarily antagonistic, not accepting of the terms and conditions as they are given, wanting to work around them, change them, challenge them. And by the way, who are 'we' really? Since we have talked of the demigods of theory, and the gods of the cloud and the valley, then we might partake of our own theological moment too.

We'd say, and this is a tease, that we are three in one – although we're certainly not claiming godhead status. We're not Trinity either, handmaid to the redeemer in the *Matrix*, and all that. However, there are three of us writing this, as well as all of those who've written into this text, informing our reading and thinking, and writing, our inscription on/as these pages. The point here is refusing a certain kind of subjectivity or writing being. It's a form of collective life and labour that is invoked, and we would like to think differently about how this life could transform itself, and how this kind of collective could make new (kinds of) writing machines. We're up for all kinds of writing by all kinds of hands; there's nothing normative about six-handed, machine-assisted, remote and co-present, argumentative authorship. The steps and feet of our writing machine, meanwhile, are never divisible into absolute authors – or individually authored book chapters. This isn't an easy undertaking by the way. We are writing as not-one, and not-many, writing over words on the page and writing in new ones with each pass; we each bring differences to the text.

The differences are significant. As Hélène Cixous and Catherine Clément found when writing *The Newly Born Woman*, in 1975, a book whose shape was governed by the 'hellish/heavenly' dance of the tarantella, collective writing is fierce. They wrote about the structures of language, writing women into place. Perhaps we three, writing together, move more freely, our respective roles unclear also and unclarified, because Clément and Cixous danced for us, in turn. We do not presume to mimic them but, finding ourselves in maddening times, we inherit the need for mad dances and for the writings that evince and explain them. Our writing too goes outside and inside the law, unevenly and at will, between theory and fiction. It is both desiring and declarative, a contradiction we have not sought to resolve. With Cixous, we distrust the identification of a subject with a single mode of discourse and with Clément, we see no reason not to steal the masculine declarative discourse ('speaking in order to be right' as Xavière Gauthier put it – adding 'how ridiculous!') from men. There is not one feminine, unfeminine, post-binary feminist writing, and other kinds have not died off. On with the dance.

But – before we do – that other connected word: the paean. Well, we're not saying forget it. But, in case you thought it was, and since we have raised the question of gods, this isn't a hymn of praise, or a song of songs. Still, we might save something of this theological moment – a kind of appreciation. We appreciate all this digital stuff. We live off it. And we want it. So, no caves, no absolute idealism, and no primitivism, no return. We are not trying to live without this stuff (if that were possible). In many ways we like it. The question is what to do about the terms of use, the cost, the contract, and the architects – how to disrupt their plans, distort their blueprints, find ways to redline something different. Or rather produce some other, more ambitious, possibilities to think with, some horizons other than the one that simply says more – but often means more, much more, of the same.

So, once upon a time that isn't post-digital.

The story might proceed with questions about this world:

When is once upon a time?

The time that we are. We do not offer a metaphysics of the coming post-digital. We don't even like the term, although we recognize it has some traction for a moment. It is just a label that fits commodity time. What about other times, and what about other ways of having, being, and negotiating the pervasively digitally technologized time that we are in, and the time that we are?

Can we get out?

Yes and no. We'll say more about this later. Yes has something to do with figuring other times, other futures, and how to get to them. And also with finding other ways of having, being, and negotiating the time that we are/in as well. No has to do with escapism and the idea of an untainted, unmediated elsewhere. An escape to where 'out' is would be a destination rather than a negotiation, and might be only possible in the imagination.

In a time of whatever (and wherever) media, running away isn't really an option. If Cinderella had sold the slipper on eBay, bought trainers, and skipped, where would she have gone to? The chip in her skin, the smart technology in those new shoes, and the cameras in the walls would find her. And global coverage means there's nowhere to go, at least in terms of an escape, no go-to place. No outside.

If Cinderella stops polishing the windows (servitude is the new leisure) and instead breaks the glass, trying to find the real, what happens? She finds herself back in a world she was in already, the anthropocenic, massively mediated, nature/cultures, data worlds, smart cities, smart natures, smartly controlled futures and spaces she was trying to get out of in the first place.

Oddly enough this place she left and found herself back inside, is also a kind of outside. There are the objects you'd expect, the string, the sealing wax and the mountains; although none of them as sharply outlined as the demigods expected: For a start, even if she seeks an unmediated experience, eschewing collective advisors for her mountains trip, there are her own perception filters; she may be a cyborg but she still needs ears to hear, and eyes to see, even if they are prosthetics (you can't audit that distant hum directly, or without listening).

The point about this environment is that it's real enough, but it isn't immediately available at all. It is massive and massively mediated.

Cinderella stays with mediation. Nothing appears to her without being made communicable. A new or old world is not conjured from atoms, or quarks, or geology, or imagination without processes of communication, pictures, language, forms, connections, negotiations. We've said that. Although . . . Cinderella eschews such purifications. Meaning was never perfect; meaning and mattering always slip and slide but you have to grab onto something.

What's the story?

The story takes on all the reasons to be writing, and steps on through smartness, intelligence, control, catastrophes, mistakes and revisions. The point of our story is to queer their story.

How big is it?

View does not give size, and we reject the scale division that says the big is for the big boys, and the small is for the women. You can start with Cinderella's feet, with her face up against the glass, but you can end up with questions concerning human futures, even as you reject the human as the obviously right, or obviously irrelevant, scale. Cinderella might be a robot, she's made of particles, and bacteria; she is not cute. She might be us. She's miniscule and she's giant. She matters.

Is it a game?

Yes and no, and as much as it ever was. Play is important, gamification is distraction. Gamification is TED-thinking writ large, a playable data set for global warming, algorithms and avatars with solutions for earthly survival. Big ideas are reduced to computational logics, and thus render-able to commodity forms. The scale-effects of the post-digital are weird, like ships in bottles or *Gulliver's Travels*. This is the wrong end of a telescope; as a thousand digital historians have it, this is the macroscopic. The whatever-digital wants to retain a sense of where equivalence and recapitulation end, and where they intermingle. Scale is an actor.

Where does it end?

Not with the post-digital, or any other posts. The post-digital leaves no space for any kind of future tale, and this is why we reject it. We want to write, build metrical structures, in ways which allow for the fact that the future is not yet written out, in which there is time for intervention. A tale for the time being that time currently has no time for.

Resolution versus solution?

The point is to write into the whatever/wherever digital, to look at our condition now, as a problem between its sociological and philosophical sense. So we write against the solutionism that is currently pervasive. Socio-philosophical problems cannot be engineered away, not by data, not even by the perfect visualization, that each time it is delivered suggests the same solution: the technological fix, the fix we are supposed to need. Such problems cannot be resolved by any technology that promises, simply by virtue of being, to *be* a solution.

Enough of the Q&A. Let's proceed by way of statements:

HERE ARE SOME THINGS DATA CANNOT DO

There is no technological quick fix for age or ageing, no geo-engineering out of climate change. The feminized robot caregiver and companion, which privatizes what was supplied by family or state, and was meant to be a fix, is no less subject to breakdown than its human progenitor (as many feminists have already pointed out). If you think that's what Cinderella had to become, by the way, think again. Cinderella became a data pirate once she lost her looks and her feet swelled, though she may do double time – carer by day, pirate by night. By the way, she loved her sisters, and never thought them ugly.

WRITING CANNOT BRING SOLUTIONS EITHER

But it can be powerfully performative. Moreover, it can demonstrate that there is more than data, and more than a game here. We are writing back to an invented feminist genealogy of writing that has no essence and is not an ontology. That is, it is not what writing *is* but what it shall do, what it might still do towards the possibility of remarking and remaking our time, that matters.

What about our unforgivable lack of transparency, our allusive gestures, and our lack of full citations? Forgive us. Writing doesn't always do transparency, unlike glass. It makes meaning, takes up time, does something else. Citations pattern in particular, operate in specific ways, making trails that are counted, valourized and used to define fields. In response, we have decided not to cite very much at all here in our paeon. We allude to arguments in the field and problems in the world, but we refuse to name the names in the theory canon, which even in arguing against, we would reproduce.

At the same time, we know we need to be more than gestural. But this doesn't have to be undertaken through detailed refutation. Our point is to challenge some general positions, and to produce something new. Our hope then, is that through the labour of writing itself, we give traction and detail to the issues we address.

We are remembering/insisting (again) that writing can produce the possibility of change, that it is not a promise broken. We are no more post-writing than we are post-digital. Writing is precisely working, laboring (in) the in-between. The labour of writing is embodied, situated and micro/cosmically libidinous. It has no endgame, no utopia, no political fix, but holds open the possibility of change through insurgence, antagonism and intervention. Writing as the principle mechanism of de(con)struction allows us to project out of an increasingly powerful projection.

It is because we want to let writing speak, rather than seeking to speak with a single sovereign authority, that we, the authors, write from and for a perspective that is not and never just our own. Our hope is that writing as we/I/me we can find a scale that refuses the natural scale of authorship or the single, embodied, fully human, sole author. Refusing scale, we also want to refuse the bounded-ness of traditional authorship (which is precisely what canonical citation valourizes).

We are writing for and as ourselves, and as noted, writing as three white middle-class, European women. We inevitably reproduce inequalities of representation and voice. We know we are not innocent either: to write is to be embedded and situated where we are, we recognise our own commitment. However, we are also seeking to reach out to, be in dialogue, combine with, others who also want to – or who are – writing against a rightness that is based on masculinism, manifested as scientism. We write therefore, as an invitation to engage as we/I/me/you/others? We are lost without the will and wisdom of others – particularly people arrogantly and prematurely set aside by the privileged.

WRITING IS AGAINST RIGHTNESS

The new worlds dangled in front of us these days – of big data, AI and machine learning – come with new demands to recognize what has come as what will come right. Solutionism, in particular, claims a new form of right; that not-to-be questioned rightness that comes through running the numbers, as if these were universal or – by the way – god given. This kind of rightness has no language, or so it is said. Or rather language isn't needed, is just a gloss. Solutions are solutions. Yet there is no data cloud

· without digital waste, no sweatshop-free wearable tech, no flat ontology or list of smart glass things that is not a story told from somewhere.

The point is to make a new cut.

LABOUR AND LEISURE: OUR WORK – CUT OUT FOR US?

Feminism has found fertile grounds to ask new questions, by rejecting a system of values solely based on the value of work. It always asked about the relative value of reproductive and other labour. Now it can inquire once again into the end of labour itself, since now the end of labour, when the divide between so-called serious work and empty leisure collapses, is once again being predicted. The problem of labour and leisure has always been seen to be a women's question too, by which we mean that the stakes have always been different for women. This time around, we could ask about those digital housewives, about work's intimacy, new sex work economies, uneven, discriminatory and ghost work environments. Federici long ago called for a re-evaluation of household labour. Today, others write to celebrate the radical possibilities of the end of work in a world of expanded automation. This, they think, may produce new scales, kinds and multiples of automation, including emotional intelligence, intelligent intelligence, abstract calculation. We like their voices, we like the way they laugh; we salute their Medusian qualities.

Thinking about labour, we explore what it means for women who want to undertake the work of writing, when writing itself becomes fully automated (it was always inscription anyway, remember), or at least this is what is offered. To go back, what does it mean when/if a machine takes over that distance, the distance of a breath, between thought and word, so that the distance between speech and quantification fades? It is easy to wish for code, or code intelligence. We should also recognize what it is about writing that code sets aside, or automates, so that which was a laugh that echoes, becomes an instruction to undertake.

We're not against instruction. But we *want* the labour of writing. We want to claim inscription as a means to make marks, to claim prospective futures, as well as inhabit a now. We want to become embodied (and augmented) writers in process, not still bodies accruing inertia while the world changes; the old still points in the turning world, or the deadly spin at the center of centrifugal worlds. So we don't think it's time for another manifesto of unwork. (Although we have got a lot in common with a series of feminist manifestos).

We think rather that there is space for another feminism to manifest and perhaps through a different form of writing. Our feminism entails thinking about new economies of expertise in which automation enables new forms of writing, new forms of labour, or can be/could be made to. If we're working not ending work though, can we still have a laugh? Can we still be scornful? Can we still (also) mine the furious laugh of Medusa?

OTHER GODS

What did Medusa do? Why as a god slayer, who made a flying horse, should we talk about her? If we do, should we worry that turning to classical myths in order to talk of something in a new world and place is a demigod strategy? Maybe, but precisely because of those other invocations of grace and fury, we want to turn this way, but make the turn differently.

There are reasons to love Medusa, as Cixous did, and one of them is a sense that the laugh refuses to be inscribed in one way, but also refuses speech. It is excessive, it does deliver what it promises, but it does so at the same time as taking it away. Cixous' writing delivers meaning, but provokes you to laugh. Compare with asemic writing which pleases but withdraws the meaning it promises. Laughter as a form of continuous writing, at least as we see it, doesn't reach out to reach to the impossibly receding object, nor turn back towards itself, but is always in process. It contains and is the promise. It is itself a mediation of affectivity and intent.

So, once again, we can mine the laughter of Medusa. Our writing wants to articulate the furious laugh of a gendered political subject, trapped between two horrifying myths or between a rock and a hard place. Let's get out of here!

How do we reconcile Cixous' laugh and cry with the assertion that we are beyond the human entirely? We don't. Instead we recognize with Cixous that we are beyond reconciliation, not beyond the human, and we reappoint a political theory predicated on conflict. We are using Medusa here not only to hear her laugh, but also to think towards a different kind of antagonism based on interpretation, affect and a sense of the computational. This is different from . . . terminating communication . . . unmediating the world . . . or stripping out the symbolic from the material worlds we make.

A PAEAN FOR THE ANYTHING DIGITAL

Our paean for the anything digital is provisional, a conjuring of others, more of a potion than a prescription for the future health and well-being of those whose perspective is not the default.

We recognize, but will not be reconciled to the fate that the architects have in store and the demigods don't in the end contest – enough. We sing from a hymn sheet that we are rewriting because it is not our own. Our paean reflects the mess the peon is in. It is annotated like an early manuscript or multiply track-changed. It will not get finished and nobody will 'accept all'. It is less of a work and more of a working out, a process of experimenting and opening. It works against the deceptive rhetoric of openness and transparency (open access, open source, the closed circle of our financialized knowledge and creative industries, and also against citation circularity, which finds itself trapped in ever smaller circles, an echo chamber that does not break out).

You can think of it as science fiction, as a techno-story or as theory practice. We are practicing theory practice in lieu of claiming to be right. We do not have an alternative techno-story or feminist science fictional future that is not already implicated in the present. Our dream worlds are wrought from dissentions in which nightmare worlds fracture and become disordered and incoherent.

That other theory – the post-digital post-human – is a fraudulent figure and a familiar one, drawn from the omnipotence fantasies of yet another set of demi-gods who remain stubbornly invested – psychologically and culturally – in habits of splitting and projection. The post-digital post-human is a symptom of paranoia, a post-cyborgian successor: dalek as data. Exterminate! Really – is that all we've got? It is surely rather late in the day for such tedious imaginings.

Our paean is predicated on the need for maturity – better late than never – understood as the ability to assimilate feelings of ambivalence towards the object. Good or bad, technology continues to be fetishized as an object detached from the social body. We (hereby) refute any and every so-called philosophy or politics of technology in which the object continues to function as either the good breast or the bad.

We would rather think about how objects are neither good nor bad, entirely, but how they are often unreal, or imaginary. The more unreal, the more imaginary, the more vehemently their reality is asserted. These objects are given to us as essentials: essential for something. They are also seen as essential in that even as their specificity is insisted upon, they retreat to become essences; the mountain and the computer, data and/as the ultimate in materialized abstraction. If you want to talk not about correlationism, but objective correlatives, here is one. Data as the ultimate virtual object, at once virtual in a material way, and material, in the context of abstract realms. Our paean for the anything digital doesn't want to deal in these unreal divisions, but it does want to look – hard – not at the promises of monsters (we know how to do that, it's been done well, and done in), but at the always already broken promises of unreal objects.

UNREAL OBJECTS

Below is a list of unreal or fantasy objects (also real) that precede or just short-circuit the more demanding task of assimilation. In case you are wondering, we don't think they are good or bad. The point is how they are deployed, how they operate, and how they are understood:

actuator
algorithm
ambient intelligence
ambient media
augmented reality
avatar
base pair
big data
camera
clone
cloud
computer
data
database
data viz
de-extinction
driverless car
drone
environment
energy
entropy

extinction
genome
glass
glasses
god particle
grid
hadron
helix
hologram
information
infrastructure
internet
invisible
media
mobile
motion detector
network
open
predictive
quantum
quark
robot
sensor
smart
system
ubiquity
wearable

The story that is currently being told, the *his*tory of architects and demigods is about (some of these) objects, environments and materials as things in themselves. These things are often supposed to tell themselves, to assert and affirm their potential or their *potentia*. It appears as if they do get to choose.

This fantasy does not escape the problem of knowledge, of mediation. It remains structural even as, or especially as structure is elided by scale, epistemology by ontology, discourse by materiality, the ideal by the real. Perhaps we should revisit the question: what is the relation between objects and knowledge, events and their mediation? Could we start (again) with the inseparable? With the inseparability of these pairings? Think about the god particle and the recreation of the Big Bang at CERN. Think about the atrocities at Abu Ghraib, the rescue of the Chilean miners; a flu pandemic, Ebola. Things in themselves. Mediated things? In what sense?

If it makes sense to bring in physics, biology, geology, virology and so on, it makes *no sense* to do so at the expense of the arts, humanities and social sciences. If it never made sense to speak of the annihilation of events, the endless deferral of history, then we should not ignore or seek to transcend the grounds for its re/enactment.

What are we to make of smart worlds and cloud worlds that seem so accommodating and ethereal, so willing to serve and so far from servers, strip mining, fossil fuel extraction, precarious labour and industrial farming? They are the axes of un/endurability, of good-bad paranoia and also of reparation. Big-small, unreal and destructive worlds can be cut down to size, given a sense of perspective, rescaled and re-dreamt so that the menial, mundane and everyday is less distant from the prospect of global communication and cosmic connectivity.

The point is to stay with the trouble mediation brings. We can refuse its terms of letting meaning disappear. We can see it as non-essentialized and materially powerful and we can keep an orientation to and desire for meaning-making and intervention, and attend to rescalings to account for position. There's nothing finished here. Our paean for the post-digital is a provisional techno-story of re-imagined objects, knowledges and worlds. A series of uppity bits of writing.

2
Scale, Subject and Stories: Unreal Objects

We are not anti-computing. We do care about things – but not things that 'just are'. So, our work is to engage with the gendered biopolitics of an increasingly computationally infused life after new media, by which we mean all of the technology and all of the life.

SCALE: GENOMES

The genome features in our list of unreal objects. In the new technological realism, new fantasies arise; promises of precision editing and recombining at the level of the organism. Genomes carry much of this, and futures are imagined in which genome sequences are the media of future lives, of preserved species and post-humans, aiding de-extinction, genetic engineering and cryogenics alike. They emerged as promissory things, big data, biomedical hope and hype in the 1990s and onwards. Currently genome projects refer to the existence of hundreds of thousands of genomes. Genome projects have scaled from one to many, from the one universal human genome to the existence of hundreds of thousands of genomes. Over the last few decades there has been a lot of attention to the way that information and data could be understood as exponentially more intense and more relevant to biomedicine. New big data discourses, repositories, industries and infrastructures have emerged, including grids, clouds and internets of things. Genomics is both driver and beneficiary of this emerging infrastructure. New generation sequencing drives demand for genomic clouds. Genomes are media all the way through, they exist as digital media artefacts in sequence data and the patterns of light refraction from which sequences are derived. There is no analogue genome, it has no materiality outside of computing infrastructure and no one can see a genome except as instantiated in media form. Rather like the God particle and other big science entities.

Genomes then are quite nicely naturecultural, making life that is already mediated. They bring to the fore issues of scale and the question of how much capacity humans have to understand what they do. They can't be used as the material ground of nature, although they are invoked as such in current forms of foundationalism, nor are they only symbolic or machinic. They are biodigital artefacts, diffracted light patterned from tissue, flesh, life itself. Bios recontextualized, they are intensifications of genes, previously imagined as distinct entities, base pairs of As, Cs, Ts and Gs, unseen but materially effective, units of inheritance. They are media forms transmitting messages about life to life, unseen, powerful scripts, poetic imaginings, dominant tropes of centuries of biology, codes and informational agents.

Genetics became genomics through the Human Genome Project of the 1990s; a global big science project focussed on the challenge of sequencing the human genome. At the start of the project the scale of the genome was unknown but a single human genome was forecast to be unfeasibly large. During the course of the project, the genome got smaller, sequencing techniques got faster, and data storage became more compact. The unfeasibly large got a lot smaller. Genome projects used to be singular – The Human Genome Project; now they are multiple with names such as 1000 Genomes Project, Genome 10K Project, and 100,000 Genomes. *Genomics England*, is part of this formation. It is a flagship UK coalition project that aims to sequence the genomes of around 750,000 UK patients. It puts NHS money in the hands of shareholders of sequence companies and promises health benefits for the people of the UK from genome sequences. It employs advertising agencies to engage patients and publics.

By the time the human genome had been sequenced in 2004 it was evident that the project had changed sequencing technologies from an army of *ad hoc* machines that took a decade to sequence a single genome, to a near monopolized market sector of new generation machines that could sequence thousands of genomes in weeks. It changed the understanding of genetics (single genes) to that of genomics (whole organism genetics). A proliferation of contested terms including epigenomics (which focusses on changes to DNA and proteins in one generation that are then passed onto others) and postgenomics (things possible since the publication of the genome) has chattered forth. Genomics has also positioned specific industry leaders in new markets for multiple genome projects; *Illumina* for example, which has the contract for sequencing the *Genomics England* genomes, is part of a small group of companies with a global monopoly on sequencing. Genomes themselves became less important as entities on their own. Just as everyone was promised their own personal genome (to paraphrase *Depeche Mode*), they dropped in value, both in terms of meaning and money. The big data era of post-genomics came into being, but at the same time its key terms remain contested. In the leaps from genes to genomes to epigenetics, it is still not clear what the genome (or even the gene) was to start with, but that doesn't seem to matter. Contemporary genome projects are no longer about single genome sequences, but about the generation of multiple genomes into collections that require annotation, curation, storage and analysis. At the time of writing, there are at least three big science projects running currently where the aim is to sequence 100,000 genomes, indicating that this measure of 100,000 is the new threshold for a meaningful data set (*PGP, 100K Genome, Genomics England*).

Genomics England aims to sequence 100,000 genomes and build a data infrastructure of 30,000 core processing units and 30,000 petabytes of storage. This kind of description demands some detail. How big is a genome? What kind of scale is a petabyte? They are both beyond human scale perception and a petabyte, as measure, is quite hard to imagine. There are numerous expert discussions of how to make this kind of measurement analogous to something discernable. One explanation is that a petabyte could store 2,000 years worth of MP3 files; a soundtrack for two millennia. This abstraction is another imagined dimension and will have changed as soon as I have written this. Dimension increases forwards and along. It doesn't translate this smart world into a perspective, but the idea of a soundtrack for two millennia helps to evoke the scale of ambition, well beyond the human, and a technological after effect echoing into a long future.

Genomics England is about generating and processing large amounts of genomic data (30,000 petabytes) at an industrial scale. The project is explicitly described in terms of industrialization in its promotional materials.

'The 100,000 Genomes Project is similar to the railways in the Victorian era.' The rather nostalgic claim here is that a new national economy, as well as new benefits in health care, will be generated by the project. We see in this harking back to the Victorian era, a resonance with a steampunk aesthetic; the latter entailing a shift in time that makes an out of control (technology) graspable in mechanical ways, at human scales.

More directly it is also suggestive of industrial communication infrastructure, nationalism, colonialism and empire. The claims for new economies and revolutions in health care made for *Genomics England* are similar to those claims made in relation to the Human Genome Project, from which this project spins out. The Human Genome Project has also been folded into images of national achievement for both the UK and the USA. For example, through the representation of John Sulston, Nobel Prize Winner and leader of the UK work on the Human Genome, as a UK national hero, nailed into the wall of the National Portrait Gallery – truly seminal in this one instance.

Through policy documents, press releases, popular science writing and media framing, the Human Genome Project promised to transform biology and what it meant to be human. It was also to provide benefits in health care, and social transformation through new bioeconomies. Benefits in health care have been very slow in coming, and nearly 20 years since its completion (and over 30 years since it started) we are in an age of austerity and economic recession. At the same time, we can still afford genomics. (*Illumina* was offered tens of millions for the contract to sequence the *Genomics England's* collection.)

It is tempting to connect genomics and industrialization, to draw analogies between the clouds of smoke, fog and smog of industrialization and the new clouds of computing. The smoke cloud so iconic of the Victorian railways, factories and homes became a visual signal of the devastating effect of industrialization on air quality, culminating in the concentration of smog in cities. In turn, this led to clean air acts in the UK in the mid-twentieth century, and some of the proposed agreements to challenge climate change are an ongoing attempt at the same project of cleaning up after techno-science. Recent moves to try and establish a right to clean air (Client Earth) are a direct address to this. The cloud of the computing industry is metaphorical in the sense that it means storage on some other ground-based, ground hogging, servers. But it brings its own environmental destruction, and like the smog of another century its ill effects and benefits are unevenly distributed and durable over time, place and population.

Large-scale genome projects, big data and cloud computing are part of the conditions in which people live. Indeed, the industry of genomics has driven the demand for massive storage and cloud solutions. However, the touch of these conditions is felt very unevenly across different parts of the globe, and different populations and identities. The industrial scale of computing infrastructure brings with it world-changing conditions, or at least exacerbates the conditions of industrialization.

The technological cloud has become an everyday trope, offered to audiences through advertising, promising empowerment and efficiency through cloud computing. Talk of the cloud travels in trade and technology discourses. This cloud has antecedents in terms of how the digital is imagined. A history of terms like, the ether and cyberspace, conjured an immaterial other space where things could float around. Media history points to the ethereal and other-worldly imaginaries attached to electricity, telephony, photography, sound and film. Cyberspace has always had connotations of a transcendental, heavenly and immaterial realm. Reworked as a web of communication in the 1990s, this imaginary leant itself to a more mundane register. The branding of 2.0, social-networking platforms and evaporation of cyberspace made things less cloudlike and more grounded, at the same time that the language of the cloud became an explicit marketing and technology discourse. Transcendence became more pragmatic the more it became embedded in genomes, cryogenics and space travel.

Can such epic and destructive worlds be rescaled and re-dreamt so that the menial, mundane and everyday are understood as one way to scale the prospects of global communication and cosmic connectivity? Who and what are the singularities among genomic abstractions and what is at stake in accounting for them? Singularity and the singular are curiously intertwined. Genomics discourse promises to usher in the singularity, the moment of cosmic change of such degree that the universe will change again. It scales through personal genomes to multiple species, at once singular and singularity.

SUBJECTS: LOOKING DIFFERENTLY

One approach to pulling different scales into play is to look at life stories. Genomics, although cosmic in promise, has also involved a proliferation in life stories, and genome sequencing read in this light can be seen as a technology of biography. Life, story and scale are enmeshed and taken together might generate different stories about techno-life.

One of the challenges of putting life story together with genetics is that the narrative of the individual protagonist – whether taken through patient groups, through celebrity, or though narrative fiction – is a form of individualization. But individual lives open up to multiple worlds. The company name of the genome retailer, *23andMe,* indicates the highly personal appeal of the genomic life story, shorthand for my 23 chromosomes and myself. If, as the seminal portrait of John Sulston indicates, the genome is a form of the self, then a story about biography and genomics is doubly selfish.

One way to disrupt the disjuncture of scales, between the genomic offering and the self it is directed towards through the personal/personalized/dividuated appeal, is to take an aggregate of multiple stories, to help to bring into focus the structural effects of inequality, privilege and precarity. This piece of writing is an attempt to take up critical theory and analysis, and of life story and biotechnological entanglement to works in this grain but is specifically concerned to open up some of the detail of experience and to put this into conversation with the industrial scale imaginaries and horizons of techno-science. This shares an impulse perhaps with other projects like *Telling Tales of Technoscience* and *Cyborg Lives?* where researchers looked at their own experiences to bring questions of feminist genealogies, finite witness and situated knowledge into the indefinite horizon of techno-science.

Genetic testing after the Human Genome Project draws people into biomedical projects as research subjects and objects in the name of health benefits. These projects also have the capacity to undo subjects, to cast terminal diagnostic shadows that pronounce you dead, or dying, or just to undo who you thought you were by showing that your family stories of ancestry or racial identity are not what you thought.

Personal genomics, self-tracking, genetic-testing; all invite responsibility for identity, health care, health promotion, disease management and prevention. The micro level of personal genomics is constructed as a component of big data systems in which the individual is positioned as both agent and beneficiary. In this discourse of DIY health care and personalization, participation is conflated with individual agency and autonomy. As a contemporary paradigm, this sounds promising on a general level, but at the level of the detail of the rituals and choreographies that people are caught up in, it feels different.

Katie King uses the terms 'scoping and scaling' in trying to take on some of this complexity. Entanglement, drawn from Haraway in King's work, there becomes a framework and approach, as well as an ontology: 'Scoping and scaling keeps relocating the agencies we have even as we discover that agency and control are rarely at the same scale of analysis'. Scoping and scaling are active terms, forms of doing and process.

This piece of writing is also an attempt to rescale, and as part of that it also attempts to produce a certain disorientation. Disorientation might be a way of shifting focus without de-contextualizing; a disorientation is always relational; Bodies are bigger than genomes at the same time that genomics is an industrial infrastructure. The shifting materiality of the cloud, the scale and scope it evokes, helps also to provide a sense of what it means to experience and trace the touch of genomics in everyday life at the same time as being overcast by its shadows. Disorientation is thus here a way of grounding ourselves, and locating visions of both techno-science and media theory in the particular.

The point about individual lives is that they are not one, not reducible to pre-given ideas about (genomic research) subjects, citizens or states. What the life story tells us is that paradoxically, like Irigaray's sex, which is not one, there are not singular lives. The singular and singularity combine, and explode indefinitely outwards, rippling into futures, populations, technologies.

And also into writing; This book moves in and out of the 'we' of the authors and indicates other collectives, supplemental to that of the authors of this writing, probing another sense of connection and offering a collective bonded dimension to individual stories. The originary subject of this story is a collective whose composition changes over time. Katherine Hayles starts her story about a history of computing by writing that 'my mother was a computer'. This puts women into the history of computing in a strategic way. My mother wasn't a computer but became sequenced and I'm putting her into genomics in another way. My mother died of lung cancer or perhaps the wrong genes, or the smoke of the railways, the smog of another century, the commodities of the tobacco industry, the asbestos of the buildings she worked in; any or none may have conspired. She was also a mother, daughter, sister, wife, lesbian, catholic, social worker, traveller, reader, writer, listener, opera lover, enemy and friend.

I started sharing a house with my mother in 2010, the first time we'd lived together for 20 years. We rented a large town house in Brighton that could accommodate three generations. She referred to herself as the granny in the attic. Soon after moving in, she had issues with balance and vertigo, and generally not feeling great. Maybe the attic was a bad idea. After a few consultations with the doctor, a range of tests were ordered.

Mum went into hospital for a couple of days to get everything done at once. Many tests later she came home.

Some weeks later we met an enthusiastic consultant who explained that spino-cerebellar ataxia type 6 was the problem. He explained that this was a newly identified condition and had been discovered during the course of the human genome project, that it was a CAG nucleotide repeat, an autosomal dominant condition. He said that there was nothing that could be done about it, but that there was very interesting research in this area and if mum would like to join a research cohort there were opportunities. In the meantime he said that she should come back every year to see how it was progressing. My mother did not find this to be a particularly illuminating interview but we were both reassured that we knew what was wrong and left with an appointment for her to return in a year.

Recently, there have been claims in relation to *Genomics England* that it too has enabled new diagnoses. These new diagnoses, like those of the human genome project of the 1990s have been heralded as evidence of the radical promise of the genomics project to effect treatments. However, even the most positive commentary in the company press releases concludes that the most significant outcome is certainty. Now patients and families know what their condition is called; that thing that is haunting their lives, it has a name. Certainty might be helpful, but diagnosis and treatment are not the same.

To come back to a story, my sisters and I (all in our 30s and 40s at this point) started to think about testing for ourselves. Of three sisters, two of us decided to have the test and one didn't. We both tested positive and genomics became both less abstract and more menacing. My own personal genome suddenly seemed as creepy as my own personal Jesus – *Depeche Mode* again – but still as unreal.

In the meantime my mother's balance and general health didn't improve and she never really seemed to be able to shake a cough. Through that summer she was coughing a lot, very fatigued and, on uneven ground, her balance was really unstable. Her doctor sent her for an x-ray. The diagnosis this time was stage four terminal lung cancer with six months to live, possibly longer if there was a positive response to radiation, lung draining and chemotherapy treatments. During the process of this diagnosis another consultant accessed the x-rays that had been taken in the first round of tests, over a year earlier. It turned out that although the tumour had been clearly visible, no one had attended to this information at the time. It appeared that once the genetic consultant had seen the interesting genetic result, the results of the other tests had not been taken. It might, or it might not have been possible to prevent the cancer from killing her had it been picked up a year earlier. Lung cancers grow very slowly. When we instructed legal advisors to pursue this question, it was the view of the medical trust concerned that curative treatment would have resulted from a diagnosis at that time.

MISTAKES, MISTAKES, MISTAKES

This is a story of unpromising mistakes, of some things brought into focus and other things left hazy, missed and mis-taken. The registration of the genetic glitch led down a narrow path; nothing could be done about the condition it produced. The other glitch, which occluded the x-ray, prevented treatments from opening up. The management of media materials opened some pathways and closed down others, neither glitchiness nor seamlessness made much difference. So here is a story which finds its force in relation to a single, unitary body. It is about how a person's length of life might have also been cut down to size in direct relation to the promise of genomic futures.

Health these days is supposed to be all about the digital, from sequencing, to diagnosis, treatment, patients, instruments, populations, infrastructures. Promises of an age of information, access and participation have facilitated the idea that DIY health is about empowerment, for both patients and health workers. Access to information as a resource for making informed choices in relation to health care is assumed. However, information about genetics and genomics is of indeterminate value and has an uneven relationship to knowledge. Evidence of a novel genetic condition, about which nothing can be done except to join a research cohort isn't particularly helpful to a patient reporting symptoms that impair quality of life. Participation is not agency. Access to information is not the same as knowledge about health.

Genomics has been very effective in reframing biology as genetic, in producing new genres of genetic narrative, in identifying genetic conditions and in generating faster and smaller sequencing and storage technologies. It has not delivered on health care in terms of treatment or cures – and neither has it produced the predicted national economic boom, although there have been profits for many. There have been other large-scale national genomics projects since the Human Genome Project: DeCode, Generation Scotland and private initiatives such as the Personal Genomics Project. These projects have developed, outsourced or purchased high tech sequencing and storage technologies, produced samples and data and posed challenges about how to manage, curate, interpret and annotate data. Big data expansion; beautiful patterns. They have not to date much improved health or drug development. Tests for genetic mutations such as BRCA 1 and 2, which demonstrate predisposition for breast cancer, have been costly and tightly controlled. The debate around direct-to-consumer genomics has coalesced around a temporary consensus that this is not medically relevant information, yet.

A lot rests on that 'yet'. It is a promise we are given that genomics will become medically relevant. It is an aporia, a promise and – so far a vacuum. Yet, *Genomics England* has been allocated millions from the NHS budget. This 'yet' connects the mundane everyday of collecting health data with the imaginary of global, seamless and interoperable databases delivering revolutions in health care and new economic utopias.

Yet, there is little money for basic health care or reduction in patient waiting lists. 'Yet' contains the meanings of 'so far' and 'at some future time' together, lending the present to the future. It also contains the sense of 'but' or 'nonetheless', which makes its temporal promise nebulous. I am not dead yet; genomics hasn't been radically helpful in terms of health benefits yet. Will both of these surely come?

The Human Genome Project mapped the human genome and identified or confirmed disease genes. This increased the number of genes that are known to be disease locations and led to a proliferation of genetic tests. The production of the genome as a digital artefact and the proliferation of tests, fuels the demand for petabytes of storage, and for data curation. It has not had much impact on treatment or cures. At some point something will come and it may have been worth it. Either way, future treatments and cures will be storied as triumphs without much attention to the losses that came on the way. The Human Genome Project and its successive 100,000 genomes projects are too big to fail.

The human genome project, with its nod to the human, the individual, turned out to be about information processing, sequencing and storage. It operated as a site of media proliferation in which signs from biological samples could be remade as biomedia, which could then be taken to be an expansive site of meaning making about people. Where it made disease identifications, it generated tests, which in turn generate more information, as well as opportunities to patent the tests. This generates research activity, but rarely returns to *the everyday life of people in all their human vulnerability*, except to identify them as having genetic mistakes, as potential research subjects, and/or to sell them individual tests. Tests generate more information, but not the wisdom to act. Information overload is added to under-resourced health care environments. Health care professionals and patients are increasingly asked to make decisions on the basis of increasing amounts of uncertain information with a tenuous connection to knowledge.

Information and knowledge are not the same. To have access to information about something is not necessarily to know about it. Information is framed as useful *per se*, and as interchangeable with knowledge. The offer of access to information is conflated with agency, but to know something requires attention to, and interpretation of, information. In the case of my mother, genomic information was attended to and contributed to knowledge of a genetic condition, but it overshadowed other information (expressed symptoms and the other test results including the x-ray), which were not attended to until much later. Knowing about the genetic condition didn't turn out to be very productive, and information about the cancer tumour sat in a file for over a year before it contributed to any knowledge. *So much for the subversive power of the glitch.* The choreography of media forms, information and knowledge are an important element of how these gendered biopolitics are enacted in direct contradiction to the promissory rhetoric of empowerment and benefits in health care.

Media forms co-exist and are interdependent, and although the promises of information and data offer utopias of friction free communication and information, these are entangled and complex. My mother's body was the subject of a variety of tests and medical instruments in the attempt to make her readable as a patient. Parts of her body were extracted and diffracted, through taking blood and exposing her to radiation, to make her intelligible in the register of possible diagnosis. Those processes made her a medium of information about health, a medical subject. Texts were produced during these processes and people made interpretations at multiple points in the circulation of those texts. The messages taken from the texts that resulted: x-rays, sequences, reads, print outs, labels; were read and interpreted in different ways. Those interpretations were used to produce other texts: letters to the patient; emails to consultants and hospital administrators. Those interpretations were also used to make judgments about who would see them and when, and when and where they would be filed. The circulation of those texts, the infrastructures used (Royal Mail, IMAP, POP3), the order in which they were distributed and received, the attention paid to them, the subsequent interpretations, all had bearing on the meaning making and relationships between information and knowledge. Databases of disease information, medical journals, national health services, Wikipedia pages and patient support groups contributed to the processes of making meaning for patient, consultant, family and friends.

Assumptions and internalized norms about vulnerability, age, race, gender and expertise also played out in communicative environments, especially in face-to-face consultation. For example, we assumed the younger male consultant was the expert about the range of tests and processes to which my mother had been subject, rather than the single test result on which he had been consulted. The first consultant we saw assumed he was the expert but didn't know which patient attached to which texts; the second consultant we saw assumed that we knew nothing about genetics but decided to explain the results in technical terms and encourage us to volunteer my mother as a research subject.

This is not a piece of writing against biodigital culture, or materiality, but it expresses some anger about the over-inflated promises of techno-science and its occlusions.

This writing is more particularly about how the inflated promises of techno-science are part of the politics of everyday life, but paradoxically also get in the way of that life. Groups identified as making genetic knowledge – research scientists, consultants, geneticists – are attached to particular narratives of expertise and progress in which more genetic research is a common sense goal and genomes are the currency of promising biomedical science. Those whose lives are represented as the beneficiaries of the biodigital gift of genomics, its sequences and databases, are sometimes made invisible. Indeed they may be undone by being subject to such gifts.

INFORMATIONAL OBJECTS

Data clouds, like the magnitude of genomic data, are not really clouds. They are servers, core processing units, pixels, screens, circuitry and any number of other bits of stuff, most of which is environmentally damaging and toxic. However, if we accept the metaphor of the cloud as the state of data storage, we could say that these clouds have shadows, and that these shadows are unpredictable in what they over-cast.

Data clouds promise weightlessness but are weighty, have heavy costs. Weather clouds, also alluring, deposit acid rain, redistributing nuclear radiation, fall out, ash and pollution.

We are interested in the interplay between the evocative image of clouds as clouds, and their recasting as computing infrastructure. This interplay offers ways of thinking about the relationship between unreal objects and lived experience. On a sunny day, or looking across the sea, the shadows of clouds are visible moving over the ground or water.

You don't feel the cloud, but only of the loss of the sun. Clouds cast a shadow felt across a life, even when the originating object is concealed. We are interested in this motif as a way of tracing the touch of unreal objects such as the genome. The genome is both concealed and in the open, it has multiple kinds of materiality, although not as a genome *per se*. It is a digital media artefact, a sequence collected in the hundreds of thousands, a book (the human genome is printed out in book form in several places, one example is in the Wellcome Gallery), data points, refracted light, raw data, SNP data. It is a promissory figure, a promotional tool, a dream of a kind of universal machine for biology, a history of how biology became a techno-science.

Today, we are presented with proliferating visions of ubiquitous and mobile computing, device networks, grids, clouds and networks of things. Clouds promise to hold the world of an indefinite excess of big data and networked everything. As many have pointed out, the cloud not only materializes data, documents and files, but proliferates devices and server farms with such magnitude that they directly exacerbate issues of deforestation, strip mining, mountaintop removal, war, fossil fuel extraction, fracking and demands for nuclear power. The hardware for the impossible worlds of unimaginable and beyond human-scale data is rapacious in its demand for more resources.

One direction in the media theory turn to materialism has taken up the question of ecological cost directly. This examines the trail of residual media produced in the wake of the overproduction of devices, of disposable, upgrade cultures and the desire for more. It has also taken up the indeterminacy of matter through an attention to materialities, such as heat, and has antecedents in research on how environmental factors like air quality, pollution and toxicity might be as relevant as genomes to the health and vitality of people, environments and nonhuman others. Can we read the anthropocene as – or in – the shadow of the cloud?

INHERITANCE

My mother died at the age of 64 from lung cancer. More shadows, on lungs in x-rays, in clouds of various kinds, and of death. Her death curtailed many things; it also prevented a story of increasing deterioration due to the ataxia, and the opportunity for some of us to witness our potential futures in advance.

My mother experienced an entanglement of media forms and interpretations of her health and mortality in the last few years of her life. Experience is intersubjective and doubly mediated. It is both at the limit of the communicable and multiply communicative. Her interpretations of experience, and experiences of interpretation, were also mixed up with partners, daughters and friends. We are reading her, and this is another interpretation of her experiences and mine.

Spino cerebellar ataxia type 6 was discovered during the Human Genome Project. Referred to as a genetic mistake by the consultant, it lives on chromosome 19 and remains a condition about which nothing can be done, according to conventional medical discourses. Testing for this produced different kinds of knowledge for different people.

It is a struggle to avoid speaking for too many others in the discourses of genomics and big data, with their claims of new universals. In this book, we feel that we should try and not speak for too many others, at the same time as we feel we should avoid individualization. This story is about collectives but also specificity, individuals and contingency. An individual is always already plural: each one among and with and as all others. This story is scoped and scaled, a singular genomic cut that matters and that materializes a different version of genomic futures. Now I have a genomic life story; there is a 'me and the human genome'. Companies like *23andMe* who sell genome testing invite everyone to have 'a me and the genome' story and many people have taken this up. I have written about this take up for other people; conducted media analysis of genetic autobiography and public understanding of genomics. My genome story is very different to the genomic life stories I have read elsewhere. Mine doesn't involve interviews in the *New York Times* or science blogs, or spit parties with the digerati. I won't get paid for it nor can I claim to be part of the global science project of democratizing genomes, or even a national project of improving health care.

Although, it would be disingenuous to not put it out there that I might accrue academic capital from writing about my genome story, grist for an academic mill in which publication is supposed to prevent perishing.

However, there is a collective embrace. In the era of DIY healthcare and big data, we are all data subjects for whom opting out of participation is not an option. That we must generate, collect and curate population scale data has become a ruling ideology. This is a media life where people are identified as generative of data and the data generated is represented back to us, so that it shapes how we understand ourselves. In the short term the value of aggregate data is only relevant to those orchestrating the collection at the scale of hundreds of thousands. In the longer term a politics of the database that accepts the database, that enables data to make value with data, will come in. This computational or cybernetic process already shapes infrastructures around us, demanding systems, protocols, processing and code. The becoming of data subjects both exacerbates the conditions of big data and offers optimism and agency (or at least participation). However, the optimism of agency in the case of participation in genomics is closer to the cruel optimism offered by Lauren Berlant than the promise of agency taken at the level of promissory media discourse.

In Berlant's formulation, (neo-liberal) capitalism offers forms of oppression and cruelty, and the hope of freedom from them in the same moment. The cruelty and the hope are co-constitutive. Her formulation is bleak, indicating that for those who don't accrue enough economic capital, capitalism is doubly cruel; eviscerating life while making it just bearable by offering the hope of escape. Data subjectivity and genomic life stories evidence this dynamic. These conditions extort data production in the name of participation in the data spectacle, promising technological utopias, improved health care and infinite community. The promise of genomic data futures is inflated, illusory and indifferent to individual lives. This promise does more than just over-determine, it takes away attention and resources from the sites at which anthropocentricism might be resisted – environmental science – and individual lives might be considered – primary health care.

STORIES: SOMEWHERE BETWEEN GENOMIC LIFE STORIES AND NEW MEDIA THEORY

Texts, imaginaries and materials are too closely interwoven to take them apart again. The history of media theory is a history of partitions: media from message, text from context, material from symbolic. We read such partitions as false divisions that enable and encourage bad conceptual turns, returns and simplistic substitutions. We reject the idea that there ever was a symbolic divorced from materialities and we therefore reject the need for a reactionary reassertion of all things material. It is only matter that matters? Should we reconcile the world of things with the world of symbols? No need. No need either for the continued division between humanism and technicism, technology and use, Williams or McLuhan. Mediation is a phenomenon that demands better ways of thinking – beyond divisions and partitions. If the interwoven world of co-evolving subjects and objects, media and events, stories and stuff is its start point, it is not immune to the power that operates in re-cutting and re-ordering. Mediated worlds are by no means flat ontologies and – as we will keep on saying – they do not write themselves. As co-authors we co-author them. Meeting the universe halfway, as Karen Barad puts it, is about co-authorship and the responsible, accountable boundary work that is done in between. Meeting the universe halfway requires subjects as well as objects.

Questions that this writing project address include those of how to bring the inflated illusions of techno-science into a relationship with the mundane, how to bring a feminist sense of perspective to the hyperinflation of scale and how to attune big thinking to small actions. Not so much to get close to the metal but to get real. Imaginaries and multiple kinds of materiality (really) hang together in complex entanglements, which cannot be undone; the material and imagined are both aspects of reality and actuality and the unreal has material effects.

Much of the turn to the material in media theory is a move away from understanding media in terms of narrative and representation generating pictures in our heads. However, the move away from the symbolic is also a failure to appreciate the extent of mediation as a phenomenon that incorporates but exceeds narrative and representation in material formations. An arc *and* a machine. Media forms now no longer reside in the same shape or material as they once did. With the arrival of the algorithm, and the exacerbation of media life, more and more elements of our world operate as media forms. Genomics generates pictures in our heads, doubly so as creative agencies become involved in defining its meaning, and those pictures are as important as the material infrastructure of genomics, its institutions, sequencing machines, databases, tests and data. The construction of genomics as material is something of a feint. Genomes are only realized as media texts; they take the form of sequence data, results take written form. They have to be read, interpreted and they must elicit response.

Stories about data become even more important and they are the grounds on which the elite narratives of big data, which create a new mystique, can be challenged. The circulation of letters and their talismanic power to offer entry into interviews with consultants was the means by which my mother's genetic mistake came to elide the large tumour in her lung. The more convincing, but less real object of genomics came to eviscerate the reality of her life, as much as the more materially evident but differently invisible tumour that killed her.

Theory that evokes women's bodies but in their mythical form in fact erases the body, now nothing more than a crystalline trope of elegant theory The same bodies are dismembered by the mechanisms of techno-scientific projects in which information tends to overload materials. This is the shadow of the cloud, the cloud shadow that meant the shadow on a lung x-ray was missed. Dancing attendance on the materiality of digital culture, in the case of genomes, comes at the same time that the information produced has become overwhelming. The insistence on bringing into focus the material practices of genomics, obscures the lack of meaning; the turn to materiality forgets that the visions in our heads are still where meaning about materiality is made.

The genome casts shadows. These can be felt in terms of lived experience. It produces affects and effects: wondrous, exciting and joyful for some, evocative of fear, anger and frustration for others. It is costly for everyone at present, and profitable for some. At the same time the enthusiasm for genomics together with an ambivalence about the grounds of the project introduce a slippage between vision and experience. The vision of empowering patients with information about their genomes is at odds with providing care for impairment in quality of life.

From the impossible, human-free, eco-imaginary of clouds, smart grids and cloned tigers and other big science dreams to the actual impossibility of sustaining life in times of economic and ecological disaster: impossible worlds are a symptom of the biodigital. Funding is poured into big science projects that promise revolutions and technological fixes, while exacerbating inequality. At the same time money cannot be found for the lived experiences of everyday life, for a different kind of story, a cushioning against the viciousness of precarity, for education and for health, a liveable life.

Scale: too much, too big, too impossible, not scalable. Subjects: undone, disappeared, objectified, sequestered into impossible choreographies. Stories: the stories about how big data and biomedical promise will save the future deny that they *are* stories, but PR companies, creative agencies, media producers and publishers are employed to tell them. Storytelling can change the story, offer different connections and choreographies, rescale and offer possible subject positions and other impossible worlds. The singular is always already plural. What kinds of world are made im/possible through the bonds and alliances of singularity? What forms of being and becoming-with might (my) mother mediate?

3

Bland Ambition?
Automation's Missing Visions

PROLOGUE: THE COOKER

Here is a woman wearing an oven (Figure 1); Birgit Jürgenssen photographed herself as a housewife needing to get out of domestic constraints ('*Ich möchte hier raus!*', Figure 2). You start out with your head in his

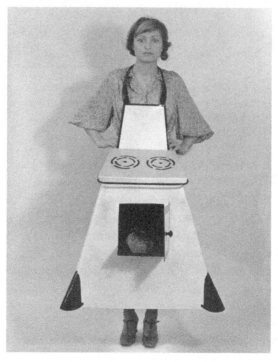

Figure 1   Birgit Jürgenssen, *Hausfrauen-Küchenschürze* (Housewives' Kitchen Apron), 1975, 2 b&w photographs, each 39.3 x 27.5 cm. © Estate Birgit Jürgenssen / DACS, London 2019 / VERBUND COLLECTION, Vienna

Figure 2   Birgit Jürgenssen, *Ich möchte hier raus!* (I want out of here!), 1976, b&w photograph on barite paper, 40 x 30.9 cm. © Estate Birgit Jürgenssen / DACS, London 2019 / VERBUND COLLECTION, Vienna

arms and end up remade as his cooker. The photograph dramatizes what was not then unusual: women cooking in 1970s homes. What's striking now is that this is a portrait of augmentation. The oven constitutes Jürgenssen's outskirts, her outer bounds; she is technologically extended. *Apron* was part of a retrospective exhibition of feminist avant-garde works of the 1970s, displayed at the Photographers Gallery in London and elsewhere. From this distance, what's clear about these works, which are by turns angry, subversive, ironic, caustic and painful, is that they constitute a serious, and seriously ambitious revolt against a particular kind of domesticity.

Now, when technological transformations of home and work once again accelerate, and when the consequences once again appear to need investigation from the perspectives of feminist thinking, the propositions explored by these women, their take on women and automation, as at once a reduction and an extension, both of freedom *and* control, have new salience. History belongs to the victors, said Walter Benjamin famously, but he also sought to explode what was repressed in the old world into the new and let it come to act again; not least to act on how the future may be thought.

So, with Birgit and co. in mind, here's the claim. Feminism can think about automation in ways that some forms of analysis deny themselves in their over-hasty divisions. Cleavages divide production from reproduction, the symbolic from the technological, material from immaterial, flesh from machine, object from representation. They are made possible by purging each side of what it contained that already refused division. Feminism, or at least our version of it, starts by recognizing that these are old and broken cuts; humans/machines, nature/culture, such cuts never stay clean, we're all already contaminated. Recognizing this seems essential to generate a techno-politics. Without it how can any demands made be anything other than one sided or half-hearted? This chapter asks what a full-hearted feminist position on automation can amount to. The wager is that it amounts to more than bland ambition and certainly more than a domestic makeover or a better cooker. Here goes.

AUTOMATION FEVER

Automation is expanding, infiltrating more deeply into homes, workplaces, cities, bodies, and transforming the infrastructural architectures that increasingly span and link these zones. *So let's begin with automation fever,* with those fevered speculations concerning the putative end of work through automation, the robotization of everyday life, the augmentation and upgrading of humans, and the automation of knowledge and expertise, that are current these days. What these speculations have in common is that they respond to a series of developments, including advances in hardware, in sensors, big data, machine learning, genomics and biotech. But they are often striking for the narrowness of their focus, addressing change in highly selective and divided areas. Too often we are given the transformation of everyday lives and places, *on the one hand,* and the transformation of labour, work, and workplaces, *on the other.* What comes hand *in* hand, is thus separated, and neither the terms of this separation, nor its impacts, are interrogated or critiqued. There is, however, no need to accept failing polarities, notably those of labour and leisure, production and reproduction, as a basis for building useful models. What falls outside the zones of home and work, for instance? Where else is there? What becomes of 'nature' in this division?

Automation is not a series of discrete operations, just as automation fever is not a matter only of technological objects and their operations, or of discourse. The traffic between digital materials and flesh bodies, between images and circuitry, code and language, all elements intrinsic to developing automation, does not follow an established route. There is no stable hierarchy of exchange relations, neither in the old base and superstructure sense, nor as this might be envisaged through newer models such as via the taxonomy of the stack. If automation processes are complex and not reducible materially, we also need to recognize that complexity has temporal aspects.

These forms and materials, political techniques, cultural imaginaries, symbols, contested and consensual delusions/illusions co-constitute temporal passages; they promise to take the bearer on, from now to what will come, and are integral in how that promise is materialized.

Those in thrall to automation fever pay lip service to the complexity of these passageways to the future, but simultaneously tend to configure them as insistently linear. The way forwards is viewed as smooth; from the smart home to the really smart home, from the augmented to uploaded smart body, from home robot to self-aware clone, from work to the end of work. These passages might be daunting, but they are not, in themselves, so very difficult to thread through; or so those enamoured with computational automation as progress tell us. It's just a matter of following technology, or being cradled within it, of taking those big steps forwards in its arms. It's always *forwards* in these accounts, and 'forwards' moreover binds technological advance with more forwards-looking, and faster, forms of life. Suspicions that any aspect of the future may be *less* – less interesting, less equal, less just, less viable – don't find much of a place in this strain of automation fever. Moreover, there are wayfinders to help, groups such as those at Oxford Martin in the UK, betting on singularity, and their counterparts in Silicon Valley, for instance. Then, on the left, there are the accelerationists, whose paeon to think tank inspired Universal Basic Income (UBI) as a new form of populist utilitarianism often has all the appeal of a middle management Powerpoint, and who seem to think all that is required is a form of post-agonistic common sense, and some efficient leaders who can ensure the 'most advanced' technology is put into full and most beneficial use. This is as far from a new 'commons', by the way, as it is possible to get.

The persuasiveness of these easy paths to these near futures can be maintained, so long as the nature of their facticity is not explored too closely, and so long as their costs are not explored beyond themselves. We need to be more aware of what we are walking on, when we take some of these passages into the future; spoiled lives, precarious labour, industrial dreams, imaginaries, projections, actually existing developments and the legacies they prescribe, technicist over-excitement, amongst other things.

Some passages are dead ends. Some of what has been carved *out* might need to be caved *in* before new routes to really new places can be found. Some of what attaches to you, you may want to discard (and this may be harder than you thought): us too.

So we don't want to take the path of automation as simple progress, (or presume it's easy virtue, come to that). However we too want to generate 'ways' to respond to automation, and to shape the social form it may take, the forms of life it may enable, and recognize our own place within the broad milieu we have just described, at least in the very basic sense that we think automation can be used for good. Good for whom? And in what way is good the real issue here?

We recognize that the new spirit of automation seeks to be ambitious: to augment, advance, accelerate – all that. Through the agency of this a-list, taken up by the industry, and also pounced upon by some left automation advocates, we are promised new things: notably new homes, and increasingly, new lives beyond work. It is easy to doubt how realistic some of these claims are, particularly given the tendency to suggest delivery will be complete within tightly constrained time scales. Evidence justifying scepticism might be found in the fabulous and specious forms of what is widely given as 'already nearly' reality today, in marketing material, or design prototyping, for instance. But this isn't really our focus here. Our intervention focusses not so much on whether these futures visions are sustainable, but on whether they are ambitious enough. Or in some respects ambitious at all. You don't have to reject ambition *tout court*, to question the trajectory of a particular *form* of ambition.

What's missing? Amidst all this prophesized social change to come, these so-solid promises, under-pinned by gadget-scale instantiation, algorithmic advancement, proto-typical experimentation, hard investment; there is one relation, one form of life, one series of relations, one intersecting bundle of identifications and positions, that often appears obdurately unchanged. Why is the 'nature' of family life, the sex gender relation, the question of labour and leisure as a *gendered* relation, the question of women and women's normative role – all the subjects of feminism – so often set aside from, or excepted *out* of all the projected turmoil new waves of automation are going to bring *in*?

MORE OF THE SAME?

Evidence of this exception is all over the place. Here is just one example, a vision of what might happen under the roof of the smart home of the future, as it was liberally (natch) described by *The Guardian*. Here is the new technologically defined western domestic. It includes the architecture and the devices (communications, waste control, power management, sensors everywhere, new kitchen units) and a standard family unit; two parents, two children, two bedrooms, detached. Here are Peter and Jane and Mum and Dad. And here, in an illustration accompanying the story is the 50s-style family so lovingly mocked in pastiched Ladybird books (the original insect media, in case you hadn't noticed), which the latter also celebrate, with all the necessary irony to make them highly marketable, their own heteronormativistic past. If that's not a word, children, it is now.

We might have expected more from *The Guardian* than what amounts to a slightly nuanced version of a well known corporate vision of the near future; a Corning Glass video presenting a day 'made of glass'. In Corning-world, the home has become transparent and intelligent. Its dividuated inhabitants are 'there for each other' as they are each prepared for their hard working day, and flash glassy smiles all around. Corning woman, at the centre of the home, is prepped for work as she brushes her teeth, while Corning father serves breakfast in the Corning kitchen. Of course Corning Woman is not 50s woman, nor even 70s woman. But you could say she's not really very different, she's just been added to. She's the responsibilized, professionalized, upgraded version. Madonna, whore, *and* professional worker. She is just as joyous (jouissance-full) in the labour of scrubbing (teeth) as any French theorist could wish, and now that her actions can be fully captured to reveal, if not her unconsciousness, then any retrograde instincts, any pesky old lack, can be addressed through predictive environmental modulation. What's new here is home technology, social relations remain unchanged.

PLATFORMS?

Of course, it's easy to object that the Corning glass people, and *The Guardian* lot, and others showing us popular visions of the future, are dealing in images and representations, in what is not real. The point insistently made by object oriented theorists, is that it is the technology itself and its operations that is important. Their call is to turn away from representation and focus instead on medium effects and operations, on algorithms, code, platforms, architectures, *substance*. This enables the discarding of revenant discourses with their tired presumptions. Representations of the future, such as those given to us as narrative films, or media stories, are seen in this light as neither informing, nor powerful, certainly compared to what will be imposed or determined by the computational itself.

So let's look at what medium technology serves us up as, how it produces the kitchen of the future, and genders it. This takes us to a Google search for the intelligent cooker of the future. You may try this at home – but we have a search we prepared earlier. What does a search engine do with a cooker? First it threw up a series of links to actually existing appliances, somewhat limited in their range, and strangely devoid of future appeal; kitchen units to come with rather gender neutral affordances. But then the gender switch switched back on. No more standalone kitchen units; instead I am served up a *Guardian Labs* advert that tells me what (social media platform) algorithms made of me.

COOKER FACES COOKER . . . AND BOTH ARE TO BE IMPROVED

I have been categorized 'woman' through the virtue of algorithmic classification and am invited to align my sense of self (and/or self worth – my prowess) with a woman seen kneeling at a cooker. I am indeed invited to bow at its altar. I am to seek to be a domestic Goddess, to channel Nigella *and* Donna. I have simultaneously been *coded female* and addressed or treated as such. The neutral automated sort is not one. You knew that, of course. The germane point here is that this imposition of gender is as much about algorithms (and their medium effects) as it is about representation (and symbolic power). There then, already coded into digital networks, is the same old, same old, social ordering, the old gendering. Women, it seems, are still to be improved through their embrace with a cooker. The automated future (and/or visions for such a future, or predictions about what it may be) will not be free of such categorizations. Automated categorization, *already* operating to shape what is to come, is already operating along 'traditional' lines. This is a sinkhole around which sinks much that is hopeful, interesting, or ambitious, about the prospect of new augmented, speedier, accelerated lives, it gives the lie to the claims that they are 'automatically' better. So many future visionaries, proud of their progressing gadgetry, with a sense of deploying revolutionary materials and designs, are oblivious to the possibilities that might arise if human-to-human relations also transformed, and are certainly not designing technologies to overturn rather than automate further 'traditional' forms of life.

This produces a future that is, despite its shiny gloss, profoundly conservative, one that operates largely within 'the most narrow parameters of change'. The phrase is from Audre Lorde, who described herself as a 'Black lesbian feminist socialist' and questioned how a movement could call itself revolutionary, if it operated only within such parameters. It is used here with some caution. Lorde was explicitly referring to feminisms' failure(s) to think enough about race in the second wave, and this is returned to below. Here it's used to link revolution, ambition and the technological. Talk of technological revolution is cheap. What would it mean if digital technology was exploited to genuinely socially revolutionary ends? For instance if those moulds dividing humans into binary (ternary, quarternary, or even intersecting) groupings, those categories that overdetermine relations across the vast field of human actions, were not simply re-divided, re-poured, and re-set, in new technological conditions, but broken utterly. What if something new was fashioned?

Considerations of how to be ambitious for feminism specifically through technology have been undertaken before, of course. Notably the feminist Shulamith Firestone, operating around the same time as the avant garde photographers producing the works that accompanied *Apron,* fought to ensure that the new forms of media technology of her era were taken up and used to generate female emancipation. Firestone wished to liberate women from the sphere of reproduction *tout court* and is most notoriously known for her advocacy of artificial wombs as a means to end divisions she viewed as imposed by childbirth. More rarely remembered, but far more interesting, and revolutionary, is her demand to use new technologies to abolish sex as a generalizing cultural category, a sort-tool for everything.

Firestone's perspective, notorious at the time and becoming even further out of joint as post-feminism took hold, might have renewed salience today. *New Statesman* and *Atlantic* reports, for instance, have both noted that Firestone's automated birth techniques now appear far less outlandish than they did, as emerging developments in digital biotech 'catch them up'.

A somewhat different issue is how her more basic arguments about the sex/gender relationship and the role of sex in culture now resonate. Here it might be tempting to argue that Firestone's time has both come – and gone. Automation and developments in computing in general that is, might be rendering Firestone's project obsolete. This argument says none of this pesky division-between-humans stuff, the stuff Firestone campaigned against, matters any more, or won't in the near future. The advent of full automation, so it is claimed, will mean that nobody's arms will be in anybody's sinks any more. Devices with anachronistic acronyms like MAIDS (Make All Incredible Dishes; the queasy servant terms remain, indeed multiply, and look at their gender), and their descendants will do all that work for us. The rapturous reception given to rumours Apple's Siri would become embodied, stepping out of the screen to stand by our sides implies we want this badly. And soon too, so the threat/promise goes, work outside the home will become an exception, a labour of love undertaken by the few, rather than the central organizational principle of a gendered (wage labour) society. The fourth wave of automation is on us, enabling widespread extensions of cybernation in industrial circumstances, and the rise of intelligent robotics mean machines will take on many care functions, as well as much of the load of administration or middle management.

Viewed from this perspective, it's easy to see why Firestone's demands look like they're about to become obsolete. The demands they made, the political programme they promulgated will be at once delivered on and rendered irrelevant. Or so we are told; you may have doubts. We do. A certain basic scepticism is necessary about the prophesied timetables and plans for the practical implementation of the general passage out of work, given that they are drawn up by automation's most passionate advocates. It is germane to note here that the ILO (International Labor Organization) believes that the biggest single coming change to women's place 'in the workforce' globally will be a shift *into* organized (paid) work, rather than out of it – we are just saying. On the other hand the belief that material changes and computational advances will rapidly produce new

mechanisms for living, and perhaps also new forms of social organization and everyday life (even if, as we've already noted, these are not the
shifts shown in the popular previsions), is shared by many, us amongst
them.

But again, disputing the prophesied speed and extent of automation,
seems less important here than disputing its purported power to pain-
lessly eradicate earlier distinctions, thereby delivering to feminism, a
classic and terminal 'fix'. This is the new old big mistake. The claim that
automation itself, by itself, can render irrelevant or engineer out older
distinctions, old questions of difference, and that it can, therefore, *render
feminist techno-politics itself irrelevant* is dangerously complacent.

As well as widespread.

That is this basic claim is evident in much writing dealing in the big
myth of terminal work automation and it is often also found in strong
singularity and human upgrade discourses. More 'modestly', but per-
niciously, it pervades solutionism as an ideology of big data (where
patterning and calculation and not ideology is said to be determinant,
and where human perspective or situatedness is seen as a variable to be
adjusted rather than a basic condition for the production of knowledge).
Notoriously, there is *Wired* magazine and its acolytes and apostles calling
out the end of theory and the end of speculative reasoning, or hypothe-
sizing, in favour of induction; note the patterns in the tea leaves, a cuppa
spat out by computer, and don't worry about whether they make sense,
simply make it your business to observe what is shown or displayed.
Applied to social questions, this says that automated accounting always
knows better, that big data patterning automatically takes priority over
rich description, and the former and the latter are divorced utterly. We
can also find this position 'in the flesh' where it says we are going to be
augmented, automated, uploaded, and that in skins-beyond-bodies, or
bodies-beyond-flesh, we'll be beyond all that caring about this division
or that one. Finally too, there it is in labour as automation brings about
the end of work and the working life and so an end to all those discussions about work hierarchies, glass ceilings, race, gender and first and
last ins and outs, and an end to those gendered divisions between home
and work.

It's not that these social relation questions don't appear in many of the
automation intensive discourses. They do, and they also often appear in
the theorizations underpinning them. But they don't have to be acknowledged as mattering (as much) any more. They are not a key issue in a new

world where computer epistemologies and knowledge productions can, so the argument goes, increasingly wipe clean old guilt by reprogramming old mores, automatically. The point might be that these divisions are now nobody's fault, and nobody's responsibility to care about, since it is the disembodied and abstract logic of computation and automation that will order the new and post-political forms of social order. Technical media 'determine our situation', said Kittler. No they don't.

THE POLITICS OF TIME

Asking if, or how, we can keep hold of Firestone's ambition for a post-gender society, means thinking about time travel, or the politics of time and memory. Feminist ambition is tied up not only with what is inaugural (more of that below), but also with what we have already and want to keep or discard. What kinds of imagining, ways of living, ways of seeing, learning, knowing, what assumptions, presumptions, mores, are caught up in the arms of automation so that pipelined, projected, transplanted, they arrive, mixed up, but still potent operators, in some future to come? If some of the given passages into an automated future we are offered today are sinkholes which sink hope, as we've said they are, then how do we construct others, how do we negotiate through them, and what about the baggage? What tags along without being invited, what should be left behind and is not. What is our allowance?

There's a version of technological time travel we are very familiar with; nostalgia and media technology have an affinity. We experience it in film noir, late post-cyberpunk, steampunk and contemporary material culture. Partly because of the purchase of nostalgia we're already familiar with many of the objects that land, higgledy-piggledy or in neatly ordered heaps, in visions of automation in the near future, such as those that give us Corning Glass time, or *Blade Runner* time, or hipster time (the latter supposedly skips slightly ahead of mainstream time by skidding back behind it). Nostalgia gives us old dial-ring telephones, vinyl, record players, typewriters, LPs, polaroids, nostalgia-inducing objects, coming from the 60s, 70s, 80s, and/or referring back further in retro-retro design circuits. These of course hold echoes, resonances and desires for old lives, old social relations, or for old temporalities, which may remain held, or which may escape. Medium nostalgia is a kind of time travel, but does not seem apt here, in this exploration of automation, gender and home.

We'd rather travel somewhere else, in some other way. For example, by re-invoking Birgit, and the call she made in the early 1970s, which was to reject the device, to resist the cooker, and to do so through an aesthetic engagement with her own situation. Birgit's augmentation became her, but she didn't want it to, she wanted to get out. Feminists exploring augmentation today, and also questioning its terms, need to do the same, perhaps. Even if they're not intending to stay there, it's a strategy, or perhaps a game. If it is, then the aim is not simply to chase the new, which then turns out to be old, nor to let the old social orderings back in with the new (technology), but to get out, to break down old borders, find new cuts, and inaugurate something else. The need is to find a way of thinking automation that shatters these conservative visions of the visions of the future and exposes their faux ambition, and exposes the algorithmic activity that produces my interpellation through code into an aspirant domestic goddess as non-innocent and non-essential.

If time travel can help to do this, it is not that version which mines the past for comfort, or which brings into the now objects indicating stable human technology relations in a changing world, (how easy it was to master the old devices, and how central mastery was in the old relations). On the contrary, the return is made for ideas that can explode any comfortable sense of progress and/or progress's path. These ideas just won't fit. The encounter today, between feminism and technology, in the context of social power and injustice, has moved on. But there is recurrence here; feminism *confronts* computational technology as Judy Wacjman put it long ago, or *enters* into a love relationship with it, or *avoids* it, again and again. So why not learn from this history, or rather let it become powerful again, rather than either forgetting it over and over again in the ecstasy of the new, or dredging it up, as dead object to be entirely the plaything of the present. If it's a game, it's a serious game.

GETTING OUT? AND HOW TO?

The question to be put then, a feminist question, is how automation can help in any projected feminist escape bids? How, that is, it can be used to free us, rather than bind us in more tightly to unequal gendered relations. We have already argued that feminism can help in thinking automation differently, precisely by refusing to accept what the current offering offers as ambitious or radical. In this way, it can identify those forms of conservatism at the heart of technological change that blunt the latter's potential to be radical, and it can refuse what is labelled as having ambition, but is offered with this dull heart, and demand something better.

One of the annoyances of constant declarations of the all new, of technologically given revolution, is the rise of a kind of jadedness towards the future (that's the sensibility of the post-digital if you want to give it a name), an incredulity towards the meta-narrative of technological alteration that comes at the same time as this narrative is established, normalized, has even become a genre. Incredulity mixed with resigned acceptance then; many automation stories, this time around, have this feel. They share in the peculiar bathos produced when the announcement of disaster opens into the horizon of banal normalcy. 'The Fourth Industrial Revolution is here.' 'Nanotech will change the world.' 'Donald Trump will end it.' Meanwhile, since you are at an airport, flicking magazine covers, why not just buy a handmade flapjack; it has 87 ingredients, and will last forever being essentially fossilized, but is saved from the bad, and might even save you from the bad, or so we are told, through the labour by hand that went into its making. (We never meant that kind of labour, nor that kind of valourization, nor that kind of 'by hand'). Questions of labour and issues of attention/distraction go hand in hand. They are often articulated as forms of myopia; we are invited to think small and walled about this stuff. Small in the sense of confining your thinking to how it affects you, small in the sense of defining who 'your' 'community' is, narrow – or short-sighted – about where the real effects, rather than the putative benefits of automation, might be felt.

To question the future that it appears technology will deliver isn't to turn away from technology per se (on the contrary), nor is it to doubt technological developments will arrive and will be significant. The further automation of expertise, the automation of intelligent control, the gathering, sorting, ordering, linking, joining up, the processing and acting, the modulating, and organizing, is real.

The issue arising once again is where this process takes us, and where we want to go.

Suppose you do want a home revolution, but don't want to be Corning Woman? Or *Guardian* ladybird? Suppose you don't believe that this is an option for everybody – a universal option – but is only available if you happen to be the right person, crossing the right intersections, at the right time. Suppose you think it costs too much? Suppose you thought digital technology could help humans along a trajectory where gender is less important and central, but your mobile, or your Google maps, or your fitbit, or the real owners of these (not you, but the platform capitalists, to whom they report) *don't want to go that way.* What then? What might you/we/feminism do about it?

AUTOMATION FEVER AND ITS BINARY DIVISIONS

Industrial visions heralding cybernation of the workplace circulated widely in the 1960s, which was briefly in the grip of its own automation fever. Many of those exploring these visions, including those on the left, excluded from their consideration the experience of women outside traditional workplaces. What had been famously explored by feminist Betty Friedan as the 'problem that has no name', the boredom and misery of (some) woman trapped in undervalued domestic roles, was often not deemed relevant to cybernated idleness – viewed as a coming problem for the leisure society and its now unemployed workers. There was the abolition of work, or its termination, and the state of leisure to come, a new state for the old working classes. Into which were included, in this sense at least, all those whose labour would have ended – but not necessarily, or not in the same category, those whose labour was largely unrecognized as having begun, or as having been properly productive; women at home.

This division has been questioned multiple times, but it persists. The automation of the labour of reproduction over here, the automation of work (in the sphere of production) over there. Line up, line up – and then look at who is in which queue. Feminists have long undermined this division, through various wages for housework campaigns, via debates between radical and socialist feminism and economist and cultural Marxism, and also in the work of Cynthia Cockburn and others on gendered labour and work practices, for instance. However, today it comes tumbling back, this time in relation to contemporary automation and its spheres of operation, so that on the one hand there is the redesigned domestic, the home of the future, and on the other, those far reaching changes in industrial production and the workplace. The issues arising in each sphere are (still) often addressed in relation to different modalities; experience, sensibility, affect, on the one hand, economic analysis and political economy on the other. The 'end of work' is often invoked without question of the disruption of everyday life or home life being raised at all, let alone recognized, in a more than gestural way, as intrinsic. Yet it doesn't take much to uncover what we already knew; that there were never two sites, but only one, a Mobius-like fold, a continuum, the aristocracy of labour and the subservience of home, work and leisure, the small scale and the large; divided but always already connected.

WHO WRITES?

A complaint seems allowable here. This might be a detour, think of it as our own mineshaft about *gemeinshaft*. It concerns the gendered writing and research practices that police such divisions, maintain them, and value each side differently. So why do we have to write about the domestic side of the strip (which isn't even a side, as we have established, since it's a mobius strip)? Why can't you? An early reader of this chapter asked who we meant by 'you' here. Our answer is that there's a composite you, to be discerned in much techno-cultural writing. So nobody is intended in particular; but if you think the label fits, wear it – or cut it out and do something different.

Why do we have to write about what is proffered as the minor key in automation futures? The small bit, the not so substantive bit? Why do you pay lip service to symbols and signs, to emotions and sensibilities, to the intelligence operating the realm of the everyday, to information emerging through the study of experience, but then turn and turn back to attend to what are designated as the big questions (the end of work, the end of the human), as if those changes, if they come, are not going to entail and be entailed by all the rest; everything else, the granularly operating social order, what is here now, as new, and what refuses to be left behind and 'comes along with' to play out with the new?

There are many scholars writing and researching questions concerning women and computational technology and automation, but there are rather few men doing this. There is a politics of writing (as a labour of work) here and it matters. Invited to speak at Harvard, in the 1960s, Audre Lorde turned her entry pass into an attack. Why, she asked, did she, as a black woman, have to be the one brought in, the one to insist on the importance of recognizing difference, and the one to talk about feminism and race. Why, she asked, should she become the representative, and by being present, compensate for, or become a cover for, a more general condition of absence. Why should she do the work of gathering a resource, of identifying experts. As she put it 'am I the only possible source of names?' Lorde was noting the discrepancy between formal recognition and real investment. She was invited to speak as a black woman, but was the only black woman present. Her complaint was about having to do the work, about *more being necessary* than a pious and token invitation to take questions of race and/in feminism seriously, if that taking seriously was to happen. This might also be the case in relation to the place of gender politics (and intersectional gender political issues) in automation and labour debates. Currently these things are often add-ons, after-thoughts. *Some automation of reproduction with your automation of production main meal for the weekend, Sir?* And how would it be to add some Afrofuturism? A corrective hermeneutics gently and silently invoked after (what is perceived as) the real matter of the real event, the place where the surplus value always was.

WRITING AND MASTERY

Lorde questioned the labour politics of certain kinds of writing (who has to do the work of finding and inscribing the names). She also asked what it was possible, as a black woman, to do in writing at all. Lorde wished to write, and wrote incisively, but she is also famous for averring that language, the master's tool, could not dismantle the master's house. This is a question still arising in relation to the work of writing and gender power (logocentrism as phallogocentrism), in relation to race, language and histories of slavery and oppression. It is made more complex in new conditions of inscription, which do not do away with these earlier issues, but in which logos combines with code, and natural language, with machine language. It was a coded interpellation that hailed me as 'woman', that delivered, to my address, the representation that confirms this ordering, and that intoned: 'bow down to the cooker, cooker'. We are already some way in to a new inscription economy.

Technologies of automation, and in particular AI, suggest this economy will continue to evolve. For Lorde, being in the master's house meant that the tools of language would always be inadequate because they were (or are) *his* tools. But computational automation, attending to questions of control, specifically, underscores the need to ask who or what is in charge, and what does being in charge mean here anyway? Automation provokes consideration, not only of masters (and women, and feminism, and power), and of mastery as a struggle between humans, but of mastery itself. What does mastery mean? From the Heidegger of the *Question Concerning Technology* to the Sadie Plant of *Zeroes and Ones* (and they were always less far apart than might be thought), a strand of thinking concerning technology has pointed to ways in which apparent mastery is revealed as an illusion; those who believe they are masters of the world through technology are caught up in their own webs, in nets they believed they spun and controlled. The necessary corollary of that being that even if mastery is an illusion, those who seek to master are violent, and use their ultimately ungovernable tools, language, writing, and their capacity to enable or withhold access to them, to violent ends.

So let's diverge from writing of one kind, and from fierce adherence to issues of authorship or ownership (whose house is this? Is code the master's tool that built the master's house), to thinking about the house of the digital, the house that computational culture built, and is building, in different ways. What we're interested in is whose house this is, understanding this not only as a matter of who owns it now, but of who made it, and who continues to build it through habitation. And we are interested in the matter of who or what might claim it, in whole or in part, if not through ownership, and if not as the master.

A conventional answer given, when the question raised is of who built our tech and tech culture, is that regrettably once again, or naturally once again (this depends on your point of view), men did. Silicon Valley is male, the vast majority of the leaders of the major platforms are male, and STEM and so forth are more male than ever. All true enough, but that ignores another part of what is essential to a building operation: the labour of making, the labour of maintaining, the labour of routinized code work, and the internationalization and feminization of labour. To set all this aside – this operating, processing, writing, inhabiting – and consider building only in terms of traditional authorship (original creation viewed as a work to individual talent) and mastery seems to us to dismiss, to elide and to lose what is contributed through what we would term maintenance, maintenance in operation and even *care*. To do so is also to think only of mastery of the thing and to ignore new questions that we need to address which concern modulation, directing, ensemble control, networked agency, co-making (By the way we're not giving away creativity, authorship, or rationality; we simply want to recognize that there is more to inhabitation than that alone).

So, divide 'control of' by 'labour to' (to reproduce, to maintain, to remake, to contribute to, for instance), divorce questions of origins from issues of mastery, and questions about who and where and what matters in automation, from what can be done with the tools it provides, and things become far more interesting.

Seen this way it is evident that, this time around and in relation to the digital and its code, stealing the tools of the master's house isn't an option *since he never really owned either the tools or the house.* This isn't a claim confined only to what is salvageable in computational technologies, to the feminist cyborg as orphan for instance, but to the whole shebang. There was no originary family master for Haraway's cyborg to break from, at least in the sense that the masters were deluded about their own mastery. That isn't to say the cyborg's leap into freedom wasn't worth it. On the contrary.

The outlines here begin to emerge of a form of feminism that recognizes sexual difference, but refuses patriarchy and/as the origin of language, and/or as the origin of (the gendering of) code. Using the tools of writing, *and* the tools of coding, *and* the resources of computational expertise (feminist machine learning?) in a work of creative destruction is not only not impossible (and remember what Lorde said of language, she belied in practice through the work she made her own words do), but practical.

Questions of writing, and who/what writes, of writing and its automation, of the automation of tools, which might transform old economies of ownership (or cement their operation more tightly) even while they force reappraisal of the relationship between contingent control and mastery, produce a commentary on the issues of automation dwelt upon in different ways throughout this book.

Writing in common, taken up as an intellectual project and a practical activity, as it has been here, produces a division of labour, a sharing of the work of finding of names, and a sharing of sources and resources. This intersects directly with what might be *made* common in an era of general automation, and with the question of how or if there can be an automated commons, explored further below.

Writing furiously also matters. The point might be to write with fury, rather than deal in Furies. No gods, but Lorde's fury. And the fury of other women; heated women remade as cookers, computers (as Katherine Hayles notes), or secretaries. Cooker for cooker, typewriter for typist; a shorthand. My mother wasn't a computer, but she was, for a time, a shorthand typist; she transcribed the word, and dealt with us and the world, at 140 words per minute. The need is to invoke a feminist fury, to write/speak against the appropriation of ambition, and the imposition of social conformity on future visions of possible forms of transformed home life, which comes about by refusing to think about precisely that cooker/cooker question; technology and life. The point is to argue against the impulse to presume difference itself is negated in coming future worlds, and to configure a horizon in which difference can be more radically addressed (rather than run away from) in these accelerating futures. The need then is to grab those tools of language that, it is true, built the house the master seemed to own – but they were never his anyway; so this isn't burglary but restitution. Once they're in our hands, we want to use them, along with other tools, to cook up some questions, and to make demands.

THE HABITABLE FUTURE?

So let's go back in to get right back out. Let's keep the home in view, but refuse the box that puts Woman in particular back in there, in the kitchen, along with Cuisine Master, Fridge and Mirror. Let's refuse the borders of the home itself, the prison house as well as haven, as we all know. As Emma Donaghue showed us in *Room*, once you open Door, which reframes the world, a different perspective emerges. It might make the future more habitable.

How to make the future habitable, or even possible? Staying with language and code we might respond to this in terms that consider form, narrative or database? Let's take the first and go back to the Corning design fiction, which stands synecdochically for many such productions. This gives us the near future of the home as a life story rooted in the present. This story is materially attached to actually developing technologies, but relies on those for its reality claims on an established picture of home life. It could be argued that the Corning ad needs the Corning family; that it couldn't tell its technology story otherwise, since *otherwise* it would not open into the horizons of comprehension that constitute the limits of the pre-visible future. You could say that the Corning ad uses as a guarantor of the inhabitability of the future, an established view, a stereotypical compression of a far fuller range of social relations, and that it is this that enables the story to open into the horizons of putative viewers. Without the Cornings, perhaps 'we' – here we the assumed audience or auditors of the vision – just wouldn't get it. But wouldn't we? It's not clear that futures collapse that easily, nor that narrative should take the blame if they do, structurally, as it were. It is the case that to push towards those binaries at the very heart of structural narratology, is to encounter accounts that make the male tale/tail the end of the tale – a peculiarly digital principle (in/out, on/off, m/f) in fact. But this was never a satisfactory way of understanding narrative. It wasn't just that it was sadistic in its cutting in and out, as Teresa De Lauretis showed us. There was a broader problem; which was that the cultural logics underpinning the production of the model produced myopia about the inevitable failure of such models to map the complexity of narrative in operation, or in context.

Anyway, the corny Corning family, just like their neighbours, the Liberal-Guardians, are apparently typical families – stereotypical representations. But typicality *is* as the cut of it *does*. What is pulled under the banner of 'the family' here is only one iteration of what might be gathered together, only one version of what of the family has been in UK or US history, only one kind of family, or one version of home life as it is globally assumed. The peculiarly nostalgically tinted contemporary family given in such design fiction futures isn't in any way inevitable or natural as the human grouping that will claim the future. In the sense that nostalgia re-invents for itself the object on which it was based, and in that invention kills the original to which it refers, it never existed except in the imaginary, which is to say, it never has, or will, exist. Family here is playing – but only playing – the natural order, as it takes in the shiny artifice, the glassy new. It is a contextualizing normativity. An easy read/write.

The argument goes that some part of the future needs to be familiar for it to seem real. But, elements supposedly introduced to make 'the future' comprehensible produce images of worlds only hospitable to those already inhabiting lives exceptional in their plenty, their entitled nature, their wealth, their normativity. Legible identification is refused for many who are situated differently.

Writing on Science Fiction has grappled with such issues in useful ways in its discussions of the supposed requirement for internally convincing 'science', the latter long said to provide the epistemological gravity at the basis of the genre. SF (and SF theory) lost its annoying innocence about this (if it ever really had it) when China Miéville and others loudly pointed out, what everybody knew already, but some had refused to really take on board; which was epistemological gravity is based on a fantasy of coherence. Donut shaped space ships, with their viable explanations for how communications jump the light speed barrier, are as unreal, in that sense, as anything else in fiction; the sex lives of martians, or the social fantasies of Le Guin's austere utopias and their gender-fluid beings. For instance, enough of epistemological gravity, unless it's recognized as fictional. And while we're at it, or working along the same lines, let us also reject the banal fantasy of real sexual gravity, as, quite frankly, boring.

What goes for the family goes for the scene of the domestic, more broadly. For those things gathered under the banner of the home, of home life, of not working, of leisure. Here is domestic life. But what about other domestic scenes, of life lived in some other way, in shared spaces, in different configurations, of dwelling in other ways, nearer an edge, nearer basic needs? Where is the sense, entangled precisely with the technologies that are offering us a different future, of the length of our (lengthening) days (in the West), of migration, of generation, or of the consequences of new forms of computationally divided time, that radically re-organize lives everywhere, albeit in different instantiations. Where is the appreciation that there are other modes and spaces and architectures of living and inhabiting, already desired, undertaken, and suffered? What is it that sees in a particular and restricted kind of domestic scene, with all its raced, classed, gendered divisions, a 'perfection' that it wishes to take forwards, to re-build, or re-articulate in a putative future where its mores and its architectures make no (more) sense (than they ever did)?

So these home automation stories, insisting on their naturalness, inserting gravity, are not necessarily desirable, habitable, or even accessible at all, depending on your situation/location and orientation. Does the failure of these tales, make narrative culpable *per se*? Clearly not, as a cursory glance at, for instance, feminist second wave fiction would point out (see the *Women's Room* for a germane example). However the dominance in these narratives of normative tropes is tiring, and so, (although we're not doing this permanently), for the moment let's ditch narrative for something else. In fact, just to try it out, let's break up the narrative, abandon representation and turn to one of those super-favoured objects of the new now.

THE DASHBOARD OF THE DOMESTIC

Beyond or before all those hermeneutic stories, all those interpretations that make of what is properly technical, something improperly socially weighted, is the call of the real. If you want to explore it properly, object orientists, would tell us, look at the algorithms and how they work, look at the code and how it circulates, this is the perspective often taken up by code studies or digital media studies. But let's be cruder still or just more base. Let's go back to the kitchen itself, to some tangible bits of future kitchen, the core of future domestic, and automated home. Here is some stuff that is close enough to the real to be making the transition from idea to product. (How much more real do you want than technology with its future promise cut out?) We've already invoked the MAID (Make All Incredible Dishes), let's add the HAPIfork, designed to be smart enough to slow down your eating, the JUNE 'intelligent oven' with its weighing top surface, the IKEA/IDEO concept kitchen, or the door in door refrigerator.

Even here, in the full fat world of heavy devices, little questions about the social weight of innovation sneak straight back in. What constitutes the 'right' speed to eat? Is it universal, or culturally conditioned? The parameters of these devices refuse to stay properly or *narrowly* technological. Moreover, some doubts arise about the kind of devices these are. Obviously they do not function only as your kitchen tools, your convenience devices, but are data capture tools that make the kitchen a node in a larger sensor net. The harder you look, the more what is proper to look at, assuming you want to stay purely technical, gets complicated. The more you try to tie them down, and box them in, the more the edges of these objects dissolve and slip away. Their outlines become blurred, and their *soi*-desirable uncomplicated functionality, their compensatory technicity, becomes more difficult to call. Is a cooker a cooker when its job is also to capture data on your cooking, and remind you to buy new tomatoes? If you accept that everything is computerized, then where do devices involved in this process find their heart; is the chip in the cooker now at the heart of things, or the chip and/in the circuit, and/in some cloud far across the network? Are humans, now amongst multiple controllers in the network, now to be viewed in technical terms too? In response to the search for the essential material, the one thing that determines, a kind of hopeless reversion kicks in, an endless drilling down towards the essence of things. Those beautiful patterns of bits are totally fucked up by real life.

Drilling out seems a more hopeful approach. Critically engaging with these new objects might constitute a kind of future-oriented media archaeological approach. This can let them exceed their categorization as simple devices, can enable exploration of their naturalized address (how they afford what type of engagement for instance), and can reveal the degree to which they are already bound up with cultural practices and definitions. This can produce a way to rethink these devices and also to understand the ways in which they (amongst other things) overwhelm the old walls of the home. Today the kitchen has become a network node, encouraging a local concentration of traffic and density and passing on information on the desires of the local inhabitants, captured through their practices; repetitious, innovative, consciously undertaken, a matter of habit and repetition. This node operates within contexts partially given by humans (the 'kitchen' as social imaginary matters), and also by machines (you have to let the operations of code, the practices of algorithms, figure too). Here is another way to find the family, caught at home, enmeshed in the dashboards of their 'own' devices. Welcome to the goldfish bowl: objects *and* symbols, databases *and* narratives constitute its more or less habitable architectures. This is why both of the latter are of use as tools with which to crack it right open . . .

THE MODE OF ASSISTANTS/ASSISTANCE

Also on the domestic dashboard, indeed sometimes helping to run it, are new modes of assistance/assistants. They come overloaded with narrative expectations. These are the figures of the new automation fantasy when it resides at home, the new class of servant/servant class.

So here is a new task: to consider the mode of assistance/assistants, to inquire into the rising labour of assistance, and question what shapes (literally) assistance takes when and as it is automated. The servant relation is house-bound, if impersonal, and thus in some way intimate. Historically, in the UK at least and in various other rich countries, a shift has occurred from the use of human servants by the middle classes to the use of personal assistants across a computationally assisted society. An account stressing the democratization of 'help' thus links contemporary developments in automated assistance to earlier discourses of labour saving, including those circulating around domestic devices in the kitchens of the 1950s, 60s, or 70s, on which *Apron* comments.

But how about rethinking that trajectory? We should be suspicious of the use of the sexed human form in the classical robot assistant body, not so much because of its putative uncanny propensities, but because of the apparent inevitability and naturalness of this morphology of assistance.

Moreover, highly hierarchical (master-slave with the gendered and raced implications this has) relations between human and machine tend to bleed into other relationships with (human) computational operators (for instance, phone company operators working automated scripts). Accepting automation as thoroughly inhuman refuses responsibility for augmented human and can constitute a strong and repugnant justification to refuse to recognize 'unwanted' forms of humanity.

Instead of unthinkingly accepting the desirability of the shift that replaced exploited human labour, as privatized resource for a single habitation with an owned object similarly bound to an establishment, something else can be suggested. Rather than relying on the 'promise' of the further introduction of automated privatized labour in the home, consider the introduction of new forms of shared resource, the potential for shared assistance, the automation of aspects of domestic work, now undertaken in common, so that this work returns to, or becomes, a common task.

Such a move amounts to a shift in thinking, from the subservient and familial relation to the operation in common. To go beyond skeuomorphic anthropomorphism is a good idea, not in the interests necessarily of interface design, but in the interests of rethinking, or seeing more clearly, what this intervention (or even infiltration, although maybe the word is too negative), into the economy of the domestic really does. And how it could be different.

It's not that devices are your friends anyway (and were servants ever truly friends with their employers?). Look at models for the servitor: the butler, the domestic, the maid, the animal. Why does 'service' need to be 'personalized' or anthropomorphized? Perhaps because it's a way of trying to persuade us that this circuitry, given to us as almost human, is only there to help (like a personal servant but without that pesky self-interest to cloud dedication). What about all the other activities these devices undertake, notably continuous informing on their owners/users/operators/friends, not in their interests, but in the interests of what might be termed the immoral economy of the platforms.

Abandoning skeuomorphism is thus useful in the interests of seeing more clearly what issues of control arise here. The complicated/complex imbroglio that constitutes the Smart House, once you take full account of its networked extensions, its pervious membranes, its extensions and introjections, makes it all too clear that one form of full mastery – by the human of the machine, or by the human of their environment – is really not available here any more. If it ever was. But mastery as a mode of control remains, after all, to be questioned. Guiltless slavery? Mastery of the half human thing? Is that what you want? Of course not, you may say. That's fine because we've already seen that mastery isn't what feminism needs to 'seek' from technology either. Which isn't to say control doesn't matter. There is no advocacy here for giving into numbing automaticity of post-masterful technology, or slopping around in all that 1990s digital sisters soup. If I'm to be post-human, I want more say in things than that.

However, focussing on thinking through (rethinking through) control, the control that computers give and take away, that automation both automates and complicates, is necessary to understand what has really changed about gendered questions concerning the home and domestic life, this time around. The current poverty of visions of what a deeply assistive dwelling, and/in a wider world could be, are poverty struck, both because we think through computational expertise embedded in the world in relation to a world unchanged, and because we cling on to the guise of x-morphic beings in privatized personal control situations (an ownership chain, a blocked chain).

A useful distinction to make in trying to think through the economy of the home might be between accounting for (which blockchain extends *ad infinitum*) and caring for; and politics might emerge as an objection to the comprehensive replacement of one mode by the other. All this, I may add, pertains also to our sense of ourselves, as bounded, our own sense of extension and automation, and our sense of how we might wish to live as augmented social beings whose apparent bodily boundaries are themselves increasingly obviously deceptive. The form of skeuomorphism that retains the flesh body in the fully artificial machine is a form of embodied, embedded nostalgia. And we have already said we need to be careful what we take with us.

IF THERE WAS EVER A TIME TO
GET THE HOUSE OUT MORE . . .

Kitchens. Homes. The domestic sphere, domestication, technology and domestication. The space par excellence that women are enjoined to write about (again, why do we have to do it?) while muscular materialism has a good old go at the workplace end of the end of work, and at the prospects for a generally accelerated culture. If we stay with the home, are we missing out on the main act? Does getting out of the kitchen require leaving those domestic issues behind? Late accelerationists, still on the left and attached to a project that desires social justice, albeit attached to a particular kind of top down, establishment-led, reformism, attack folkists for their failure to get horizontal, or perhaps as Hardt and Negri saw it earlier, to get constitutional. The charge is of pissing around playing folk tunes while the real fight (socialism or barbarism) takes place somewhere else. The same kind of judgment emerges and/in relation to studies of labour and/in the home, except without the charges of irresponsibility levelled at those who care about it; there is, rather, a kind of relief that these 'minor key' issues (the home, the domestic, and the reproductive), which must nonetheless be recognized as important, are being looked at by *somebody*. Laboria Cuboniks we salute you!

We don't see it quite like that. As we've said. But we are *are* bored in the house as it is often given to us in theory; with the house, and with the domestic, and with the kitchen, and the inglenook, and the rest. We don't know what an inglenook is. As it is given to us, as it gives itself to us, in its current and constrained version.

THE HOUSE NEEDS TO GET OVER ITSELF.
IT NEEDS TO GET OUT MORE.

As noted, it already does. Those walls are a strongly acting performative myth. The home, increasingly networked, is increasingly permeable and extended. As for its devices, and for those it homes, so for it as a collective entity. Home is permeable, shot through with holes, reaching about, bleeding in, trafficking all over the place. What are homes, these days, but clusters of signal catchers; sensor devices already mapped into pre-categorized 'areas' for sleep, for work and so forth. A less obstinately narrowly materialist outlook might see the home, as only a cut, made of heterogeneous practices involving 'real' things, objects and bodies, but in some senses too, crucially imaginary.

Recognizing this, let's abandon the given scale of the domestic and think about the home as a node in these increasingly global networks, so that its scale becomes flexible, and its operations expansive. Not fixed at the level of intimate, nor terminally related to the cave (need for shelter), the storehouse (accumulation of what is surplus), or the nursery (simple reproduction).

There are a lot of ways to do this. At this point we'd prefer a data-driven story to a home film, a list, or a deceptively hard-edged object to think with, but perhaps we need all of these; any kind of breaking and entering might do it. Turn the kitchen upside down. Rethink the fridge – for instance as a node in a global food business implicated in issues of logistics and infrastructures. Consider the cooker (yourself and the machine) as an actant influencing, at microscopic levels, global energy flows, consumption issues, policy and/on sustainability. We don't want to replace intimate questions of family life, and people with a turn to giant structures; the important things is to insist on their connection, to insist on multiple scales operating multiply.

Scale and situation. Scaling situations in which we find ourselves, we can see that we do not need to be shut in. The house is much bigger outside than in, although this is not how we generally think about it. The domestic focus on the home invites us to view it at a small scale, to see neither its extensions, nor its multiple scales, and nor indeed its sheer networked extent. Issues of dwelling are of crucial importance to the coming 9 billion. It is a peculiar effect of operating habits of division, which are gendered, that we grasp the giant scales of a network that is felt 'personally' in relation to social networks, but do not recognize this in relation to homes.

What is it to inhabit the extended home? Why *should* this be seen as necessarily bounded by the walls, even the permeable walls that enclose a divided, dividuated, nuclear unit. How about a common home? A new form of dwelling? A better idea of care? A different sense of what it means to be both a being that may freely choose solitude over compulsory connection and a particular pattern of things, and new forms of profoundly social life. We are interested in using technology to think about what can become lighter about the concept of the home, asking how it can meet shelter and other core needs, but then re-examining, possibly discarding or replacing or re-designing or relocating everything else. The point is to think about what automation can let happen elsewhere, or let happen entirely differently, or not happen at all. It is also to reconsider the full cost of 'home' – now counted as a social, rather than privatized cost, which is also of course to recognize that the social cost includes the environmental debt.

Exploring home scales can help to rethink automation, so that the habitual divisions – internal and external, public and private, work and leisure – that are used to explore its putative effects can be recognized as ideological and convenient fictions, faux cuts, although ones that still hurt. This is part of what feminism, understanding situation and location, and also setting out to disrupt what is given as the situated, can intervene in very effectively.

LABOUR AND REPRODUCTION

But let's get the house out of itself in another way too. Let's look again at that division between the labour of production and the labour of reproduction. That division that produces as specifically women's work, the full labour of reproduction. In this area women are supposed to have an overdetermined investment, one which floods across from our flooding blood and the childbearing that it may produce (or not), into the child caring that may follow, and those labours of love that attach to this, but that also lead, by this declension, into a far more general sphere. The 'labour of reproduction' or the work of the domestic, is (still) a labour primarily undertaken by women or allocated to them as their special preserve, and is configured as that which faces production and refreshes it, but that does not produce value of any kind.

You know this. But still, the declension gets forgotten, and by feminists amongst others. Maureen McNeil, responded to this when she bemoaned the narrow focus of recent feminist writing within STS, which has concentrated on women's reproduction/reproductive issues. What, she wondered, has happened to the more radical demands around technology and gender and feminism of the 1960s and 1970s? Why have they been allowed to subside, and lose their range and scope? Her point was that what was an assault on the family, recognized as that famous haven in hell but also as the site of the most closely, and tightly forged processes of discrimination and oppression, as where class, race, gender, sex and discrimination come home to roost, has become a set of feminist demands that all too often restrict themselves to reproduction and reproductive rights. The demand is for a more expanded field of feminist inquiry. Our sense is that this demand needs to be foregrounded in the context of newly emerging forms and practices and imaginaries of automation, and in the context of the changes in the scales and operations of home we are setting out here.

REPRODUCTION TO INAUGURATION?

Feminism has often found it necessary to insist on the *labour* of reproduction, and demand that this labour be recompensed. Wages for

Housework most famously made this demand, as we have noted. But who pays these wages, or recognizes this work, if work, across the board, or across the old dividing line between spheres of labour as work, and labour as home work, is largely automated? These are old questions, re-arising around UBI as unaddressed spectres. A pessimistic response would be to suggest that even in a society 'beyond work' the gendered labour of reproduction would not be replaced since it never was only about 'that kind' of productivity. The old spheres of productive labour will be automated, what the home will get, an old story this, is a little help, perhaps from machines, perhaps from machinic servants, perhaps from the newly redundant peons of old labour.

But there are other possibilities. For instance, abandon the faux symmetry that lines up 'the labour of reproduction' against 'the labour of production', which was sometimes a strategic device for feminism, but which also often operated as a kind of shibboleth to keep women on-board in the house even while they laboured *out* of the house. This abandonment becomes more essential as the home is turned inside out, becomes an extension of itself, and (at the same time) projects or introjects its own extensions into its inhabitants. So, do this and think about automation processes across the rejoined field this produces. Questions arising then, about smart devices, smart environments, sensor data and its collection, 'dividuation' of family members, and selves, join with issues arising around the nature of work, its location, its automation, and inform these issues. With the lines broken up between reproduction and production, and the public and the private, it becomes clearer and easier to see how home and work don't have to be re-computed so that they once again face each other across a ditch of scale. Instead of using scale as a divider, the point is to think with scale, and to operate at multiple scales – anthropocenic, subatomic or urban, for instance.

Moreover, refusing reproduction and production as a binary relation, which isn't easy given, the ingrained habit of making this cut can be useful in other ways in thinking through automation and its stakes – particularly in thinking about the radically new. The philosopher Hannah Arendt feared automation, and saw little in the sphere of reproduction that could encourage or enable political activity, and was in this sense, hostile to much of techno-feminism's work. She can be invoked here, if with care, and somewhat against the grain. Firstly this is useful because Arendt's sense of the active life and its components was never binary; labour (reproduction of life) and work (*homo faber*) as invoked in a discussion in which the third term is 'action', the latter designated as a form of life neither domestic nor based on fabrication, but rather based on meaningful political action undertaken in public.

This led Arendt to refuse organized labour as the site of emancipation or liberation, that place where political subjects may evolve (and in this she breaks with Marx's sense of the location of value production). This refusal itself might be questioned for its absolutism, but the intervention is nonetheless suggestive since it can provoke a different form of revaluation, one that doesn't automatically rate productive over reproductive work. Arendt's core concern was an inquiry into the political, into what the human condition as a political condition may be. She defined this in relation to the sphere of action, and to inauguration; that 'miracle'-working possibility that humans have to make the truly new. This is natality, but of a radically expanded kind not reduced or tightly related to being in labour (at work), or in labour (childbirth), but rather a question of inauguration, of bringing in the new.

For Arendt, natality operates as a means to understand the human condition. It is both what absolutely distinguishes humans from other intelligences, and is also why she is against full automation, since it is natality that is confounded by the removal of action (of all kinds) from humans; effectively this is how her own definition of the distinction between human and machine smartness is made.

Adopted heretically, Arendt's expanded sense of natality as inauguration can both address McNeil's sense of the increasing confinement of feminist techno-politics (since it breaks out of reproduction) and can help explore ambition and/in relation to feminist responses to automation. We are suggesting then, that a feminist techno-politics can now be framed not in terms of the relationship between automation and reproduction, but as a questioning of the potential relationship between inauguration and automation. Does automation inaugurate, enable inauguration, or tend to close it down? What does it let us do that is really new, that is truly ambitious? This is key to an expanded feminist politics of automation that can concern itself with, intervene decisively in, the inhabitability of the future.

RECIPROCAL ARRANGEMENTS?

Right now, when the concerns of feminism are supposedly going to become increasingly irrelevant, in the face of a new order that will deliver on its goals or render them redundant, is precisely the time, when we should think hardest about why feminism remains relevant, about how it can intervene in technological critique, and also about why it needs to think about itself ambitiously and in complex terms. There is a kind of reciprocal economy here. Thinking about inauguration – and the ambition to inaugurate – in relation to automation and its passages, can be suggestive about how to reinstitute and develop a more ambitious feminism.

Feminism too, that is, needs to inaugurate. Not in the ahistorical way that technology pathology demands, where giving in to technological advance threatens to end discrimination and freedom at the same time, and/in the same move, a move that produces not liberation but uniform unfreedom. What seems important is to work in ways that both rely on *and* question the given-ness of feminist histories and trajectories. For instance, reaching across post-feminism and back towards political feminism, while also acknowledging (some forms of) post-feminism as one of the sites where some of the issues of intersectionality did begin to be more fully opened up. Why this matters now, is that it is precisely when we are on the cusp of change, that issues of transition are most likely to be set aside 'for later' in favour of the apparently superior claims a future designated by the powerful makes on the now.

None of this stuff is simple. Let's look back a final time; Firestone's angry demand was that women should not stop when given something, and should, above all not be distracted by other calls, but should demand and focus on their ultimate goals as women. Against this is Lorde's requirement that all feminisms/feminists stop thinking in the singular about feminism and women, and recognize difference. There is no single goal for a feminism that cannot see into itself and recognize its own multiplicity. The US political activist, Angela Davis wrote a stinging rebuttal of Firestone, critiquing the latter's failure to recognize race and difference, or perhaps, although this wasn't currently a term at the time, her failure to recognize the complexities of intersection. Nonetheless, today we productively put into relation the fierce – and at times incompatible – demands of both Firestone and Lorde. Both the insistence that specificity be acknowledged to produce a discourse that speaks against the assumption of general improvement, that refuses to take technological alteration as to be passively undergone, or equal in its effects, or non-hierarchical, and the demand for concentration, focus, care.

How do we demand? We've mentioned the possibilities of manifestos, but are frankly nervous of the form their performativity takes. One of us once wrote a manifesto 'against manifestos' which felt they laboured in making their demands, now the issue might be how they race on; Gas and go. Blog on/blog off. It does seem to us that those who continue to write manifestos for a technological future should question the reliance of pro-technological critique on futurism and its writings, and question how – and why – these are so often retaken up, in new form, as manifestos for the acceleration of digital transformation and change. You are bored in the city? You want faster cars and hate women? Or you want a glitch politics that squeezes between cracks. Or do you, like us, want to entertain that 'impious hope' for the end of it all, the end of the sex gender system and/in its racialized, classed, gendered, discriminatory workings. We can go with cars, or some of us can; we're just not sure that futurist-inspired dreams take us anywhere anymore.

So let's set aside futurism and its role in feminism and go back to the main issue for us as feminists and we hope for other feminists too. Why are women's dreams set aside, and why are men's valourized? Why is Firestone (who in a sense wrote an object oriented manifesto) not more respected, despite all her many acknowledged faults, when some other manifesto writers are loved; the Situationist men who mapped Berlin in Paris, who were bored and wanted something else, but whose depiction of women was largely as boring as ever, or the Futurists themselves, with all their hatred and fear.

Come on, you might say. It has all changed since then. All the old muscle and women hate is irrelevant. Or, if not quite irrelevant yet, then automation will make it so. Your dreams are our dreams. Your wants, our wants. If what Firestone wanted was something/some world where what was between your legs and erupted from your chest (if it did) didn't matter, anymore, in 90 per cent of contexts, then yay! What we have now, or will have soon, is a matter-made world where biological matter doesn't matter anymore. So, why should your old complaints matter? What we want to say in response is that in your theorizations, your visualizations, and your making/prototyping, all these matters still arise. Moreover, you (and we) are still accountable for them, because they arise not only in your theory, but also in a broader world.

Your understanding of what 'you' (or we?) can do with this matter is impoverished, because you mistake the end of mastery for the end of all possibility of action, the end of all possibility of becoming actors for yourselves, even within a world in which there are multiple actors of many kinds. It is for this reason that your ambitions are so often reducible to technicist blandness. In the real world, beyond these abstractions, dealing with materials, symbols, writing and code inscription, feminists, of all kinds, and all classes, and in full recognition of mistakes, of difference and its difficulties, are seeking a new home in and with the computational. And they/we demand something far more.

4

Driving at the Anthropocene, or, Let's Get Out of Here: How?

We've evoked Hélène Cixous' writing, and collaborative writing as a project against writing. She writes to us what language does. Finding herself stuck between a rock and a hard place, the abyss and the Medusa, cries: 'Let's get out of here!'

Her stuckness is that of a political subject, an emergent political subject, a female, feminist subject whose coming to being is contingent on escaping, or even destroying, the phallocentric social and linguistic structures that trap her.

Cixous was writing during the 1970s, a decade recently retrospectively incorporated into the – in relation to phallocentrism, significantly named – age of the Anthropocene. The Anthropocene is the geological era that succeeds the Holocene and describes the increasingly dramatic, potentially catastrophic impact of man (anthropos) and his tools on the environment. It describes a space-time that stretches; one that led up to the Industrial Revolution and that will reach its endpoint some time after the information revolution. The endpoint of the Anthropocene is an endgame for (technological) man: either survival or extinction. There never was a technological woman. Her coming into being remains contingent on escaping, or even destroying the structures that entrap her.

This is an expanded space-time frame. Cixous wasn't just talking about the 70s, after all, but the whole of Western, masculine language and culture. But there are still (the same kind of) traps, habits of thought, expression and action. The increased urgency of climate and ecological change, an urgency that is felt, precisely, at the intersection of science and culture, the environmentally material and the socially discursive, justify a reprisal of Cixous' injunction to get out of here.

Taking this injunction seriously is about responding to the call, asking the corollary question: how? How do we get out of here? How to avoid the phallocentric endgame stories and scenarios of man and 'his' tools? How to exit the anthropos scene?

It is time to ask the how question and perhaps even to dare to answer it, albeit from here, within the anthropos scene where some of us, some more than others, remain stuck.

There is hope (if not for salvation). There are provisionally freed places of knowledge and power at the intersections of feminism and ecology, Afrofuturist, indigenous and post-colonial ecologies, ecology and economics. It is important to get to the best of these places in order to figure out how to get out of here. It is important to get to these hopeful, always emerging, soon-to-be meeting places as quickly as possible, but it is not possible to go there directly.

'There' is not there yet. A journey is implied. There, at the intersection of, for example, current thinking in ecological/environmental humanities and ecological economics is more of a direction than a destination. These are the best of places because they know themselves to be provisional. The realization of their goals (that have to do with social justice and the fair sharing of finite resources) is contingent on being freed up from divisions between disciplines and from the significant rocks and hard places that currently structure the environmental imaginary.

Let's postpone the question of disciplines for a moment. It is a big question – too big for the cumulative or transcendent strategies of multi or post-disciplinarity. Trans-disciplinarity is more like it, as Karen Barad once suggested, because it aims at the intersections, at the places and spaces in between. But it doesn't do the work of asking, again, *how*. How do we get out of divisions? How do bodies of thought come to interact and interoperate? It is a big question, big enough, perhaps to require a new modern synthesis, a new coming together – a much more ambitious one, extending way beyond the remit of the original biological or, for that matter, environmental or social sciences alone.

So what of the rocks and hard places that trap us in our present thinking about future environments and who is us, who are 'we'? There is a 'we, the authors of this book', and its various manifestos. We are also the synecdoche we's of manifestos that might need to become manuals, political subjects and proto-political subjects, living with, stuck in, and driving at the Anthropocene indirectly because, in both of its endgame scenarios, survival or extinction, catastrophe or salvation, it is not here yet. It is not here yet as a future, as a destination for all, although, for many of course, something catastrophic has already happened. And it never was here for women, for 'us' or anyone who doesn't count as the ideal subject of patriarchy and capitalism.

The dystopian narrative scenarios and central character of the Anthropocene re-enact erasures, ignoring the usual subjects and over-writing the social and ecological violence, destruction and discrimination that has happened, and that continues to happen in the name of colonialism and capitalist expansion. For many indigenous populations, as Kyle Whyte reminds us, the dystopia was then and is now. The prospect of catastrophe as 'the end' that is to come, and of extinction as the coming end of man, masks a history of species extinction, ecosystem loss, forced relocation and economic and cultural destruction that must yet come to count. It must be accounted for in other narratives and through other protagonists.

Meanwhile, life in the Anthropocene – human, animal, technological, other – is not over yet and for some of us, some more than others, it never properly began. The epoch has not ended. The sky, as Donna Haraway reminds us, has not fallen in. But neither has the threat been lifted. But the prospect of an ending, either cataclysmic or redemptive, precludes experimentation with alternative models of thought and action and, for that matter, of being and becoming. Instead of changing how we think and what we do in relation to the world and its various inhabitants, we imagine that our human life is doomed, or might not be. Teleologies (good and bad), utopias and dystopias, progress and catastrophe – these are among the structures that trap us and preclude our mutual becomings.

The worst of these structures are the moral ones, the old, biblical stories of salvation and damnation. Salvation through sustainability. Damnation through extinction. The Anthropocene, as a discourse, as a *his*tory, a story of white, Western technological man and his environment, is anthropocentric either way. Humans, understood generically, normatively (again, as figured in the name, anthropos) are both the cause and consequence of climate change. This is the case even though the causes and consequences are dealt out and experienced differentially, asymmetrically and very much according to existing geographic and social divisions.

The Anthropocene is a story with one subject. It does not deal in differences and the uneven distribution of responsibility and vulnerability. Even though it is a story about now, it is an old story, one in which climate change becomes an allegory of the Fall, the successor to the original sin and the harbinger of expulsion from Earth after Eden. We never learn.

If at times it is oriented to blissful, redemptive endings, it can also indulge in abject hopelessness, the morbid probing of the colloquial proposition that we are all, so to speak, going to hell. We're fucked. The 'we' in 'we're fucked' is not just generically, but defiantly human and humanistic. It stands in for 'it', meaning the planet. It even stands in for we fucked 'it' up. Not 'it's fucked', not 'we fucked it up', but 'we're fucked'.

In the fucked version of the Anthropocene, the one in which we're all going to hell, we tell ourselves a story about a planet that doesn't care (anymore) what stories we tell (about what we've done to it). This is a world that is already after the human, or rather a world onto which we have already projected our extinction. That, for women, for the subjects of colonialism, and for all the usual subjects, is a double extinction. Witness the anthropocentrism, even anthropomorphism here. Not just the substitution of 'we' for 'it', but the projection (of 'we' on to 'it'), making our presence felt by means of our absence.

We can tell that we're making our presence felt when we start to trouble ourselves about life and language in the era of our extinction. If human extinctionism wasn't really about human survival, why would we need an ethics of living or a new, post-human mode of address? It's not that questions of ethics and politics, language, knowledge and being are not relevant anymore. It is that they are only relevant outside of the circular trap of extinction as survival. In our end is our beginning. The Anthropocene is anthropocentric either way. The roads to heaven and hell point only to each other. Let's get out of here!

Let us be clear. Our injunction is not an attempt to escape from past or present violence. It is not a denial of the catastrophes that continue to accrue, unevenly, in the name of white, Western, masculine geopolitics. Far from it. We are denouncing the form of escapism that indulges in the end and the new beginning that is to come for white, Western man and his newer, better, greener tools. The only escape we seek is from the anthropos scene itself.

Imagine this: driving at the Anthropocene in a car, through a city. What do you see?

The 'driving at' in driving at the Anthropocene was always going to be more than a figure of speech. A journey was implied. We were going to need a vehicle. There will be no distinction here between thought and action. What we're getting at is also where we're going. If we're driving at, we're driving. We, the authors, some of us more than others, happen to like driving, and for that matter, fast cars. We are city dwellers too.

Here's what we see: three un/real objects, nested inside each other, like Russian Dolls. Three 'c's': cars, cities, climates. Our three c's sit inside Donna Haraway's configuration of command, control and communication, or, more precisely, her desire to upend it, not necessarily by replacing top-down with bottom-up forms of power and agency but rather by rejecting binaries and autonomies, by projecting from the spaces and relations in between.

Cars, cities and climates: un/real objects that interrelate. Is the climate an object? Does it come bounded in your imagination, like the chassis of a car or the outskirts of a city? Maybe not. Maybe it is simply what lies outside – and inside – the other two objects – everywhere in the air. But maybe it is also the sky that has not yet fallen in. And remember that these objects are all unreal, at least as features of progress, promises of future environments that are currently designated 'smart', 'sustainable' or 'green'.

We wouldn't want to denigrate the development of hybrid or electric cars (perhaps we would just wish them to be faster and cheaper) but autonomous cars, self-driving cars (smart cars in the generic rather than branded sense) these are far from convincing. There's the presumption, or rather, projection of autonomous agency for one thing, and then there's the doublespeak: for road safety read surveillance, for comfort and convenience read command, control and communication. Autonomous cars, so-called, require controlled environments (they are feedback systems of sensors and actuators), which is another way of saying that they fail in (real), uncontrolled environments. Not only do they require controlled environments for their operability, they call into being an interoperable transport and communications system in which cars, roads, signs and drivers (driverless drivers) – not to mention walkers, runners, pedestrians and other animals, and trees – might be measured and managed.

Autonomous cars fit inside smart cities in which everybody and everything is measured and managed. They are a nested set of horizons that open in to each other and up to the sky. Utopian, progressive and technocratic: the smart city, like the smart car (whatever happened to the flying cars we were promised in earlier imaginings?) is an impoverished idea. It is at once nowhere – unreal, unrealized, unrealizable – and everywhere from London to Shanghai and from Rio to Mumbai. The already known and examined exemplars range from Songdo City in

Korea to Masdar City in the United Arab Emirates and to PlanIT Valley in Portugal. China alone is planning to build hundreds of smart cities.

Already massively mediated through promotional and marketing materials, and modelled by IBM, Cisco Systems, Siemens and the like, smart cities of the immediate future are imagined and visualized as if they were devoid of history, geography, politics and people. At least in the iconography and planning, there is no past, no cultural variation, no conflict, no pollution and no body. The smart city is clean(ed). It emerges transcendent, pristine and operational from a cleaned up and cleaned out ground zero. It is the perfect project for a post apocalyptic landscape. Here then, is where man might begin anew. At the same time, the smart city itself inflicts apocalypse on itinerants and indigenes, on previous urban histories and rural cultures, and on people, animals and plants that are moved on, or in.

The logic of the smart city is ruthlessly logistical. It is about systems and flows and while it persists with claims of user-centrism made bogus by what is already known about urban planning, technological infra-structure and data extraction, it is for, and only for, business. And yet it is not enough to challenge, or to go on challenging this unreal ideal with reference to the dirty, messy, specific, diverse and stubbornly embodied reality it obscures and overlays. Ideal and real, utopia and dystopia, progress (green and clean) and the catastrophe figured by polluting cars in cities choked by toxic smog – these are among the oppositional struc-tures that trap us.

Smart cities are already violent incursions. There is no dichotomy between progress and harm to be had. Take Dubai's Logistics City, a logistics and transport hub that boasts the ability to process 12 million tonnes of air cargo per year, in addition to having its own staff village set in beautiful landscaped surroundings, complete with sports and leisure facilities, restaurants, shops and other services. Here, the ordered and efficient management of networked flows and supply chains is contin-gent on what Deborah Cowen suggests is the containment of labour, especially migrant labour, in staff villages and through border controls and security zones. In these security, or (ironically labelled) free zone environments, normal civil and labour laws are suspended.

In Logistics City, there are no collective agreements or privacy rights. There is no employment security and all crime is regarded as a form of terrorism. Police become synonymous with military authority and ports become self-governing spaces in between nation states. The in betweens of smart logistical cities are the cross-hatched zones in China Miéville's novel *The City and The City*; not exactly no-go zones but precisely hyper-securitized spaces of overlapping cities in which subjects stand to breach new or arcane laws (about what might be seen and what must be unseen).

The fantasy of seamless systematization, a contested ideal emerging from the integration of corporatism and computationalism (urban space redesigned for the sole purpose of securing the management and transit of what Cowen calls 'globally bound stuff'), is also a performative fantasy whose disruption, or eruption into a reality of mess and violent conflict, is already figured in the in between spaces of European ports that fail to deal with the mass movement of globally bound humans. Logistics cities overlap with the illogistics of the so-called 'Calais Jungle' and its successors, always already disrupting the erasure of politics.

How painfully apt that inhabitants of the Calais Jungle, before the jungle was destroyed and they were unceremoniously dispersed, were marshalled into renovated ship containers from their messier tents and makeshift shelters. As Stephen Graham has suggested, the politics and stark inequalities of the apparently orderly, equitable and efficient technological systems of the world are forced to the surface when inhabitants refuse to move or when infrastructure fails: when tents and shelters are washed away by rain; when the channel tunnel is closed and tourists, commuters and lorry drivers can no longer go about their business. When systems and servers fail and supplies are blocked, in that moment of crisis – which, looked at on a global scale and especially in relation to the Global South is more norm than exception – there is an opportunity to rethink urban life: as it is, as it could be.

If order and disorder, future and past, smart and dumb, clean and toxic are more entangled than oppositional, what might their de(con) struction suggest in terms of what urban life could be? If it is not necessary, or indeed possible, to be beyond dialectics in order to get our proto-political subject out of here (in order to drive at something better), it is necessary and possible to signal a rethink and conceptualization of a new, provisional ideal-real.

Part of any case against the smart city is that we've seen it, lived it, suffered it and criticized it before in the form of the rigid, functional, administrative and even autocratic architecture and urban planning of the modernist movement of the twentieth century. There is also a striking parallel between the regressively gendered iconography of the smart home (centred on kitchens, cooking and consumption) and the post-war re-domestication of women and re-traditionalization of gender roles. Part of the problem with cleaned up, progressive, smart and orderly futures is that they end up looking so much like the past; like the 1950s, to be precise.

So, here we are in the present, driving at the Anthropocene in a car through a city. We need a better sense of what we're 'driving at' as well as a better sense of direction. For sure we're headed against the flow of traffic (most of it is still coming in; we're getting out) but that isn't much to go on. We know that we are in a time, and moving towards a future that is far from frictionless. We are in cars that are getting cleaner and more computational but still pollute the air and choke up the cities, cities whose vitality is contingent on contingence, on disorder as well as order, on inefficient functionality and on the existence and mutual flourishing of constituents with very different views of what is right, fair and good in the world. What can we offer them and each other by way of an alternative to rocks and hard places?

What if an already non-homogeneous, non-harmonious 'we' were to offer a 'what if' story, neither technocratic and progressive or humanist and despairingly optimistic, but rather speculative and antagonistic, or at least, against the flow?

What if we were to retell the story of the three 'c's: future cars, cities and climates, not so much from the top-down (versus bottom-up) point of view of a master planner looking at a blank computer screen and designing a city – and the world in a city – from scratch, but from a heterogeneous, Cinderella cyborgian, machine-Medusan perspective, that of an emergent citizen, an urbane (in the sense of worldly if not polite and refined) political subject that is neither future nor past, but contingently, haphazardly present in a variety of writerly strategies? In that case, we would tell a tale like that of Mieville's Orciny, a tale between (at least) two cities and between worlds of destruction and redemption: factual, fabulous and forbidden.

We are drawn to the border of forbidden worlds and approach them with cautious abandon, wishing we could go faster without hitting anything or killing anyone, without wrecking life and lives with 4x4 fenders, CO_2 and PM 2.5: the particulate matter produced by diesel engines and associated with toxic smog in cities around the world.

Neither girl racer nor woman driver, we do not adhere to the creed of technological speed. This car is not driving us. It is becoming automated, but not more autonomous than we are. Like us, it depends on an outside world of the climate and the cloud and of other cars and passengers. Its ontology is dynamic, a continuous exchange, although the fantasy of self-same autopoietic systems is familiar. We surely relate to its desire for self-governance and enhanced self-maintenance. That is what draws us together, as if we were ever truly apart, as if it were ever about who controls who, activity and passivity, rather than a mutually transformative process of becoming logstical.

Together we may flow, the not-so seamless car careering through the not-so seamless city, under a sky that has not yet fallen in. Speaking of that, what, if anything, can cyborg Cinders (part carriage, part foot, part fairy tale, too white, though she needn't be as hers is a perpetually retold tale) make of a future environment already framed by anthropos, and how much rests in a name?

WHAT'S IN A NAME?

There is a list of synonyms for the Anthropocene and perhaps the most persuasive of them – Kate Raworth's Manthropocene and Jason Moore's Capitalocene – identify the parallel roads of patriarchy and capitalism that led us there, in as far as there is a there, a place in geological time that, for those who speak of it, marks not only the end of the Holocene but the beginning of the end of the world man made without, in return, being remade by it.

We still need a Colonialocene, marking the trajectory of colonial expansion, marking the tendency to erase indigenous populations precisely by assigning them, consigning them to a bygone era, trapping them in the epoch of the Holocene, the time that was. The time that is no more.

The imminent extinction of man as a discrete and dominant entity – it is man's dominion over nature that is, allegedly, ended – is declared, as Raworth points out, mostly by men or by the northern, white, male-dominated Anthropocene Working Group.

The irony is not lost on her, that prominent scientists debate a scenario in which the planet has come to be dominated by human actions, while remaining oblivious to the fact that the debate itself is dominated by the voices of white men from the Global North. Irony, like parody, is a queer feminist writing strategy and political method that still has work to do, not least in relation to Anthropocene working groups afflicted by a collective irony bypass. Perhaps if there was a slogan – 'It's the end of man, says man' – they might get it?

McKenzie Wark sort of gets it. She joins the call for new names and metaphors while recognizing the need to think within the frameworks provided by the old ones. She settles for the Anthropocene as a contingent solution that sort of fits, a name that will do for the time being, a bad name for bad times. In any case, for her the challenge is not so much in the name but in forging what she calls 'comradely alliances' – and most of her comrades, like the Anthropocene Working Group, are men. Her team of Russian Marxists and science fiction utopians – she puts Donna Haraway in with Alexander Bogdanov, Andrey Platanov and Kim Stanley Robinson – are brought into play alongside Paul Crutzen and his colleagues in the earth sciences who were among the first to establish the name and set the agenda for understanding man-made environments.

Haraway herself both justifies and troubles the name, acknowledging that man – precisely the alignment of patriarchy, colonialism and capitalism – has changed the planet 'forever, and for everyone', while seeking different kinds of alliances, multi-species alliances and co-evolutions that might make the world more liveable for all of its inhabitants. Haraway's name for such alliances – Chthulucene – is derived, controversially, from the fantasy writer H.P. Lovecraft's mythical figure of the Cthulhu, an octopoid monster that Haraway reads and reforms (completely, so as to denounce its racism and misogyny and turn it towards more indigenous science fictions) so that it becomes the possibility of becoming, of extensivity and what she calls sympoiesis. Sympoiesis describes a more symbiotic form of the autopoietic or self-governing system, one that recognizes more relational ontologies and ethics, one that recognizes mutual dependencies and responsibilities between human and non-human entities within an ecosystem.

Haraway's habit of figuring alternate futures through the reinvention of natural kinds and through retelling stories, in this case, of the Anthropocene and the Capitalocene, has always been predicated on the material-semiotic, the connection between words and worlds that gets forgotten if not broken in the turn towards the so-called new materialism. A characteristic of some dialectical feminisms and all object oriented philosophies, the turn to worlds without words in current evocations of climate change leads Tom Cohen and Claire Colebrook to return us to the act of evocation itself and to insist on the centrality of language and narrative to futures in which man's place is secured in all the talk of his extinction.

If there is no climate change beyond the narrative of climate change and our reading of, and writing about it, if there is no separation between worlds and words, then there is no 'our' – no 'we', no 'us', no anthropos – that is not recalled into being by the declaration of an ending.

The Anthropocene is a story about the end of man that inaugurates, as such stories always have, a new beginning. Man's salvation is predicated on the declaration of his damnation and only in this way does the human come about.

At this point, we are brought back to the concept of the Manthropocene and to the question of whether or not cyborg Cinders, our purloined figure, our feminist figuration that might yet be an indigenous person or an Afrofuturist or rather a mundane Afrofuturist figuration (as Martine Syms insists, this means she cannot be the hero of interstellar travel, or a story about the inexplicable end to racism, or about an encounter with aliens, unless of course, that encounter is impossibly hard to pull off) has any place within it.

ROLLING BACK THE YEARS – MYTHOLOGIES AND COSMOLOGIES AS GENEALOGY

In as far as cyborg Cinders, through her non-unitary ontology (becoming-with the car that was once her carriage), is doubly excluded from the planetary yet patriarchal human *hist*ory of the Anthropocene, her only recourse is to insurgence. It is not only that the Anthropocene as an endgame is not here yet. It is that she, as a subject, does not exist in endgame scenarios. There never was a technological woman. Her disqualification, the disqualification of others like, and unlike, herself, is what she lives with, is stuck in and is now driving at. We, the authors, propose that her insurgent driving forms its own kinship with the insurgent writing of which Hélène Cixous speaks in 'The Laugh of the Medusa'. Since Cixous' subject cannot speak, write, or be heard 'in the masculine', she must shatter his story and drive her way out.

On an information trip then . . . We send our Cinders back to meet her Matriarch – a machine Medusa, cyborg, goddess and monster – because she needs, as much as ever, that rebellious, indeed, destructive laugh. She needs to meet a resurgent masculinism with an insurgent feminism, and yes, a heterogeneously evolving feminine writing and female driving that will tear his words and worlds down syllable by syllable: anth-ro-pos, ha-ha-ha! The aim is not to keep her stuck between Medusa and the abyss, her rock and her hard place, but rather, to enable her to retrieve something from the encounter, something like a strategy that might get her out. Insurgent driving, as what Cixous refers to as the 'precursory moment' in the transformation of structures, like insurgent writing is all about working out of the spaces in between.

Machine Medusa gets cyborg Cinders moving in between ends and beginnings, damnation and salvation. But what else is at stake in this encounter? Two things. The first is an exchange or inversion of gods for goddesses, idolatry for deicide, a ridiculous, laughable bromance with the forefathers for an altogether more spikey configuration of monster, Matriarch and machine.

The second thing: rolling back the years to mythologies and cosmologies (planetary evolution, ends and beginnings) is a form of genealogy or knowledge retrieval – a going back in order to go forwards – that is a necessary stage in a total rethink about relations, life and the world. Cinders goes back for Medusa so that together they can figure out what they're driving at and how to get out of here. They are not alone, of course. There are others, companions. Out of her genealogy of Marxist and utopian thought, McKenzie Wark signals the need for a rethink too, while Donna Haraway, characteristically, wades in, combining a tradition of writerly feminist deconstruction (that owes a great deal to Cixous) with her own utopian invention. Her story of Chthulucene incorporates a critical evaluation of the modern synthesis, a mid twentieth-century attempt to address the atomization of the biological sciences and to rethink biological life and relations through the retrieval and reorganization of specialized forms of knowledge.

If the sciences of the modern synthesis – those that dealt with the relations between genes, cells, organisms, populations and species – were powerful, not least in generating a world of mathematical, competitive units called genes, cells etc., they were also, Haraway insists, totally unsuitable and inadequate to the sort of thinking needed for Anthropocenic, urgent times. They could not, for example, deal with symbiosis or with the prospect of multi-species co-evolution, relationality and development that has become central, as Haraway suggests, to a wide range of scholarship beyond the two cultures divide. Something else is needed, and a new synthesis is being attempted by writers such as Haraway, working in between the sciences and the humanities.

Of particular interest here are two related areas of scholarship that place themselves beyond this divide. Ecological economics and eco-logical/environmental humanities might themselves be construed as genealogies – as forms of knowledge retrieval from within the dominant fields of environmental science and economics – that pave the way for new forms of thinking and political action.

Not confined to the limitations of mythology and cosmology, to Gaia and the idea of a homeostatic, self-regulatory system, contemporary ecological economics recognizes the disruption, disorder and potential entropy generated by mainstream economics and attempts to think and model a new economics that is in a symbiotic and conceptually synthetic relation to the ecology. Presenting itself as a revolution that lost its way with the emergence of environmental economics (a field that does nothing more than apply mainstream economic theories of infinite growth and market rationality to environmental problems), ecological economics counters the ideology of growth with a sense of finitude and resource limitation and replaces market rationality with an ethics based on the mutual wellbeing of earth, humans, and animals.

The context for the revival of ecological economics is the crisis accelerated by mainstream economics: climate change, loss of habitats and natural diversity, disease and antibiotic resistance and unsustain-able growth and consumption models. Haraway's method is a new modern synthesis that draws on thermodynamics, evolutionary biology, economics, ecology and philosophy, in order to produce a radical rethinking of all forms of human and nonhuman relations. Ideas that operate in between physics and philosophy – cooperation, connection, entanglement – are regarded as antagonists and alternatives to tradi-tional notions, again, characteristic of the sciences and humanities, of duality, autonomy and mastery. Ecological economics attempts to shift the ethical and ultimately political register from one of human rights and rationality, to one of respect and responsibility towards the nonhuman world.

The ethical tenets of ecological economics consist of:

1. Membership: Humans are members, not masters, of the community of life.
2. Householding: The earth and the living systems on and in it should not be seen as merely 'natural resources'. They are worthy of respect and care in their own right.

3. Entropic Thrift: Low-entropy sources and sink capacities, the things that undergird life's possibilities and flourishing, must be used with care and shared fairly. Ecological economics is inexorably and fundamentally about justice.

They are derived from indigenous and traditional economic systems of the past and the present, systems that demonstrate the non-universality and non-inevitability of the dominant model of market economics. What ecological economist Peter Timmerman refers to as the anomalous but intoxicating dream 'of infinite progress, infinite space, and the fulfilment of infinite desires' is, in any case, dissolving among the signs of planetary distress. Fuelled by fossil fuels, this unravelling delusion is offered a reality check that is perhaps less about the finite nature of Earth and more about how this finitude provokes and enables a re-evaluation of the 'nature and bonds of our mutual relationship as a bounded interdependent community'.

While they tackle issues of multi-species justice, ecological economists, such as Timmerman, recognize the work they still have to do in figuring the nature of the individual self in a post-humanist world.

Ecological economics addresses the humanities in its attempt to incorporate ethics and in the attempt to address the concept of the human as one that is fully embedded in, and entangled with life and the world. Ecological humanities scholars such as Carolyn Merchant and Wendy Wheeler are cited directly. Indeed, the foundational agenda for ecological humanities, although established a decade before the resurgence of ecological economics, is strikingly similar, and resonant with ecofeminism before it.

As Deborah Bird Rose and Libby Robin write in their opening invitation, 'The ecological humanities work across the great binaries of Western thought', and are dedicated to 'cross-cutting' divisions that hamper both understanding of the world and an ability to act within it. There is a strong commitment to social and ecological justice and to pursuing a sense of connectivity with life and the world at a time of crisis. The longevity of this sense of crisis, its exposure to duration is indicative of events that operate across the division between nature and culture in a way that Western knowledge has arguably still not managed to do. If, as Rose and Robin suggest, the epistemological divide has always been hierarchical, then it may be even more so now, for example, in object oriented philosophies and even in material feminisms that border on the scientistic. The vehicles for rethinking the boundaries of thought itself were in place well before the end of the twentieth century – uncertainty, relationality, intersubjectivity, situated knowledge – but, having subsequently thought a lot more about, for example, relational ethics and ontology, have the object and material turns taken us away from the promise of relational epistemology and methodology?

Moreover, and going back into the institutional worlds of scholarship, is the dialogic method preferred by the founders of ecological humanities – because it opens out the possibilities of conversations between and across cultures and species – likely to succeed when the market economy that has yet to be replaced, privileges sciences (or STEM subjects: science, technology, engineering and maths) and all-but erases the arts and humanities, thereby presenting us with the prospect of a connectivity that is fraught with conflict?

The same questions might be put to more recent work taking place under the banner of environmental humanities, but largely consistent with prior work in ecological humanities. Where this is laudable for rejecting a consensual, technocratic approach to the environment, in which environmental issues are detached from social issues and regarded as an isolated set of problems to be managed or solved, it falls somewhat short of specifying how – other than through opening dialogue about differing values and worldviews – environmental debate might be broadened, recognized as a fully social debate (concerned with questions of justice and responsibility for example) and re-politicized.

Where the emerging field of environmental humanities also promises much in its recognition of the problem of compartmentalization between disciplines – especially ecology and economy – and between levels of governance, it leaves the how question hanging. How, exactly – by what means, mechanism or metaphor – does it become possible to move in between disciplines and publics? As a field that underscores, and to an extent, demonstrates the need for a new modern synthesis, environmental humanities cannot itself be a contender or a site of synthesis in as far as it does little in the way of knowledge retrieval from the environmental sciences and does not address the area of economics that is acknowledged to be so vital to re-conceiving environmental thought and political action.

Think again!

Peter Brown and Peter Timmerman's project for a resurgent ecological economics – an ecological economics for the Anthropocene – reaches out to an ecological and environmental humanities and goes some way towards recognizing the need to rethink, again, the boundaries of thought itself.

In as far as their chosen vehicle is a philosophical tradition predicated on connectivity, co-evolution and the ongoing physical and conceptual relation between human and other kinds that they still consider marginal outside of the academy (perhaps they are being timid, they refer to the work of Henri Bergson, as an example here), it is, importantly, one that might ultimately be more indicative of conflict than consensus. Brown and Timmerman's ecological economics is interventional and activist. They take, as their principle problem, how to move from a relational ethics and ontology – rooted in ideas about multi-species co-evolution, care and responsibility – to a relational epistemology and methodology where 'bodies of thought can be made to interact and interoperate'. They accept as inevitable the disruption of the economy and of the economic subject – the consumer that is also a citizen – as market imperatives are confronted with, if not replaced by ecological ones.

Otherwise in tune with a broadly ecological agenda predicated on a new modern synthesis and an 'interstitial practice of networking between knowledges', McKenzie Wark is less willing to make what, in the language of critical and political theory, is the decision, the cut, the intervention, the choice in favour of an ecological over a market-driven economy that constitutes a form of closure and is thereby constitutive of the political. In contrast, the political, for Chantal Mouffe, is precisely the ontological aspect of antagonism, whereas the domain of politics is that of the practices and institutions that organize and manage human relations.

Where Brown and Timmerman seem willing to engage both politics and the political in the long term project of ecological economics, Wark remains invested in a resistance to closure that, for Mouffe, is more about ethics than politics and avoids dealing with hegemonic struggle. Where an ethical discourse can, she suggests, avoid the moment of closure, a political one cannot. What is more, avoiding closure and political struggle is symptomatic of a tendency to valorize pluralism and multiplicity rather than 'division and the impossibility of a final reconciliation'.

Wark's ecological agenda, her desire to take on what she calls the Carbon Liberation Front, eschews agendas and the grand narratives of ecology versus economic science, pursuing instead a more conciliatory, collective and collaborative set of solutions to the problem of climate change. What is needed, she suggests, is not just a number of different kinds of actions, but also their integration. Wark calls for the design of integrated solutions, established on a collaborative basis and able to take on board a multiplicity of individual viewpoints and perspectives. Wark's approach is pluralistic; it is oriented to multiplicity and resolution, rather than to an ongoing struggle for values. In fact, Wark explicitly rejects a political theory predicated on division and antagonism in as far as it fails to recognize the feedback loops that operate in natural and social life. The challenge for Wark is how to integrate thought and action across knowledge and cultural boundaries and across scales of management and labour, of human and nonhuman subjects.

It is worth drawing attention to the difference, particularly in respect to the realm of the political, between a model of integration and resolution on the one hand, and a call for interaction and interoperability on the other. If a quest for multiple integrated solutions manifestly refuses to engage with conflict and struggle, to what extent might the concept of interoperability – a technocratic concept currently dominated, if not colonized by internet communications, management, government and industry – keep that struggle open and thereby relate the problem of knowledge (of epistemology and methodology) to that of power and the political? Can interoperable modes of thought and action remain antagonistic and politically open? And how, exactly – presuming that interoperability is, potentially, a knowledge practice and not just a metaphor for relating knowledge practices – might interoperability be achieved?

What is at stake is the efficacy of a new modern synthesis not (for us) as a set of harmoniously integrated and efficient solutions to the three c's problem, but as a way of challenging the status quo understood as the endgame of the Anthropocene or a market-driven climate catastrophe.

INTEROPERABILITY

The ability of systems, units, or forces to provide services to and accept services from other systems, units, or forces and to use the services so exchanged to enable them to operate effectively together. (Dictionary of Military and Associated Terms, US Department of Defense 2005)

Interoperability is a characteristic of a product or system, whose interfaces are completely understood, to work with other products or systems, present or future, in either implementation or access, without any restrictions. (wikipedia.org)

IS POTENTIALLY SYMPOETIC

At least, it has already been used to link information technology (plugs, standards, protocols) and systems engineering to social and political systems and to root technics in the 'task of building coherent services for users'. (wikipedia.org)

IS POTENTIALLY SYNTHETIC

Cross-domain interoperability is concerned with 'multiple social, organizational, political' and legal entities 'working together for a common interest and/or information exchange'. (wikipedia.org)

AIMS TO BE INCLUSIVE AND OPEN

Interoperability implies the use of open standards and open standards rely on consultation from an inclusive group of stakeholders who produce publicly available information for free or at a nominal cost.

IS NOT JUST ABOUT MARKET VALUES?

The primary contexts for interoperability are commercial, military and security. The market dominance of multinational corporations might be challenged through policies oriented to interoperability, but so far the goal has been to increase market competition and innovation. Can the challenge to market dominance be extended to the market and/or military per se? In other words, what other values can be made interoperable?

OPENS OUT TO NEW DOMAINS

Cross-domain interoperability is a method for allowing systems to work together. The domains in question could include organizations, communities, disciplines and other forms of knowledge and action.

ALSO MEANS CONNECTING THOUGHT AND ACTION

In direct-response services, peacekeeping missions, the coordination of healthcare across different parts of the service and climate change programmes.

IS NOT A GIVEN

Interoperability is not guaranteed. It is not a facet of semantic webs, clouds, capitalism or post-capitalism. It can therefore be contested in itself and regarded as a method and technique of communication and contestation.

'LET'S GET OUT OF HERE' – FROM MANIFESTOS TO MANUALS

'Let's get out of here' is the cry of an insurgent feminism in its encounter with a resurgent masculinism. It is what machine Medusa says to cyborg Cinders as they race through the smart-dumb, future-past, pristine-polluted city, hitting all of its roadblocks.

It is the precursor to their emergence, as new provisional subjects, into ecological and economic environments for which they do not yet have a roadmap. 'Let's get out of here' is an injunction to think and act beyond but not outside of the structures that inhibit thought and action: the rocks and hard places of the Anthropocene, Manthropocence, Capitalocene and still to be named Colonialocene. It is what you say when you find yourself in a jam. There is no sense of where you want to go to when you want to get out of here, no implied destination. At the same time, you want out of somewhere and that somewhere implies an elsewhere, another place and time, if not alternate, then in between.

This is not a line of flight, directionless, desiring, expansive, conveying nothing and nobody, the emergence of emergence. Getting out is a process that is both open and closed. In other words, what if these provisional political subjects, these non-homogeneous, non-harmonious 'we's' know where they are and that they are stuck but have a sense of direction, a desire for in between locations that are not just rocks and hard places? What if they know they are heading for those interoperable spaces and systems that should, perhaps, be better thought of and better acted on as dynamic, intra-operable spaces and systems? What if our emergent political subjects, the political subjects of manifestos, need roadmaps and manuals for navigating ecologies – including urban ecologies – and ecological economies? Their roadmaps might be as provisional as their own subjectivities are, and their manuals might be speculative, not definitive. They might depict rather than describe the environments to be navigated. They could be drafts, plans or proposals, but they would address the question that must, at some point, follow the injunction to get out of here, namely: how?

In her call for thought and action that looks again at ecological and economic relations outside of the terms of the Anthropocene (which is not, 'available to think with') and Capitalocene, Haraway rightly observes that 'Of course, the devil is in the details – how to revolt? How to matter and not just want to matter?'

So one more time: Let's get out of here – how? McKenzie Wark does not tell us. Wark calls, in the style of a manifesto, for the reorganization of knowledges that she only retrieves. Wark retrieves the forgotten histories, sidelined concepts and untold stories. What are 'we' to do with them? Wark calls for alternative realisms and speculative fictions that will undo the workings of the Anthropocene, but gives speculative fiction too much work to do, reifying Kim Stanley-Robinson's sense of intra-operability, 'his writerly problem-solving practice for combining different visions of an endurable future'. Wark rests on what she has retrieved, and where she deserves credit for asking the 'how' question, invites criticism for failing to address it: 'How can everyday experiences, technical hacks and even utopian speculations combine in a common cause, where each is a check on certain tendencies of the other?' How, indeed?

Donna Haraway is better at the 'why' question, at laying out the conditions of domination that give rise to the writerly injunction that her work has always endorsed. Haraway is all about getting out of here, and her vehicle is feminist writing in the sf (science fiction, science fantasy, speculative fabulation, so far) mode. Still, her contribution is more to the manifesto than to the manual, as perhaps is our own in this book. If the principle problem of the manifesto is its implied or defined political subject, Haraway has done more than most writers to make that subject the subject of her manifestos. Her working out of the political subject is in part a way of working out how to get out, how to write out of the hierarchical structures that contain it.

Haraway's sfs have emerged out of new provisional concepts such as natureculture, but like Wark's, they have been, until very recently, generally not her own inventions and they are given too much work to do, as if they were autonomous rather than intra-operative zones, or as if they alone were the site of a new modern synthesis. If this were ever to have a singular mode, it would become at once too synthetic and not synthetic enough. It would lack the plurality that Wark seeks, and the cap on plurality that Mouffe says is necessary in order to preserve the ontological dimension of antagonism.

In as far as we need the speculators and the fabulists, the writers of indigenous, Afrofuturist and feminist science fiction and science fantasy, it is surely to communicate with and to challenge, to challenge and be challenged by, to intra-operate with, rather than to assimilate the philosophers, policymakers, economists and ecologists. Is it surely impossible for them to make a contribution to politics and the political otherwise? It is important, as Haraway says, that indigenous science fictions refuse to finesse the Anthropocene with 'Native Climate Wisdom'. It is important that they do not integrate, but rather remain antagonistic to it.

It is at this point that the manual, however sketchy, comes into play as a form of closure. It seems that this form is being flirted with across, or possibly between ecological and environmental humanities and ecological economics, fields whose intra-operability could well be extended. In what he refers to as a digital humanities project, albeit one with a distinctly ecological, Anthropocenic frame, Bruno Latour, a longtime investigator of (never being) Modern, proffers a user's manual for an ongoing collective inquiry into modes of existence. Where his claims are grander than Wark's in that he purports to open a lab for 'new discoveries' at the intersections or 'crossings' between conflicting modes of inquiry, what he actually produces is a provisional, if extensive, report that only seeks to justify his inquiry.

The report constitutes a genealogy of the moderns, an attempt to learn what we 'have really been' in order to work out what we might become and with who/what kinds of others. It posits a choice between modernizing and ecologizing that Latour does not make and it delegates the 'how', 'why' and 'what to do' questions to the collective and to the potential users of a manual that does not get written.

The contributors to *Ecological Economics for the Anthropocene* do not write a manual either, but as well as laying out their ethical principles, they trouble themselves with the task of identifying forms of governance and mutual accountability that might facilitate a fair sharing of resources. In their contribution, Richard Janda and Richard Lehun attempt to address the question of how; specifically, how to produce global action from overlapping and conflicting claims of social justice. What they propose is a metatheoretical approach to justice, which is distinct from a pluralistic approach in that it is predicated on identifying the strengths and weaknesses of different justice conceptions and on making decisions. They argue that a metatheoretical approach would evaluate any justice conception by asking what injustices will likely attend it.

If ecological economics is fundamentally about justice, it is also about being prepared to reject forms of justice that are based on self-interest, efficiency and growth, in favour of another model that cannot eliminate division and conflict, but might be better oriented to the mutual enhancement of earth, humans and animals.

What if a revamped ecological humanities, even an environmentally framed digital humanities, was to seek out further opportunities to intra-operate? Cyborg Cinders with machine Medusa in the car beside her might just get her roadmap.

DRIVING OUT OF THE ANTHROPOCENE

A partial, provisional manual (please add)
(inspired by Martine Syms' Mundane Afrofuturist Manifesto)

1. Forget ends and beginnings. They point only to another epoch dominated by white, Western Man and his greened up, cleaned up tools.
2. Seek further opportunities for thought to intra-operate, in between ecological economics, environmental science, environmental humanities and other fields that are attempting to map out a new modern synthesis.
3. Futures are worth fighting over, so let's get on with the fight. In order that the usual subjects do not win and lose, it will be necessary to exchange progress in the three c's for a politics rooted in antagonism.
4. Utopia is not another planet. Colonial science and fiction have always been dystopias for some. Utopia is not an escape from the violence that is done, but rather, it is a process of accounting for the harms and hopes of other protagonists in other, post-colonial, post-capitalist, post-anthropos scenic narratives. Utopia is a place to start from.

5

Technological Feminism
and Digital Futures

IN THE SHADOW OF THE CLOUDS?
OR HOW WE MIGHT LIVE BETTER

We live in the shadow of clouds. There is the cloud that is at once the abstract architectures, data flows and physical substrates of an information system that mediates everything we do. There are the weather clouds that may signal environmental damage or bring rain. And we know that these systems are not separate from our activities: the earth is clouded by human actions. Then there is the cloud that is injustice – that says prosperity is experienced unequally both in terms of what it provides and what it damages, and that not only prosperity but freedom is systematically refused to many on the basis of discrimination and violence.

Clouds join, but their activities do not necessarily stack up. Clouds intersect, interact and constitute our everyday lives and our horizons, doing so in immensely complex and fluid ways. Cloud formations are in process, as are cloud relations and dynamics. Moreover, clouds have local atmospheres. There are all kinds of sectional validities (to use Fredric Jameson's very old phrase), possibilities apt and operant for particular scales, materials and conjunctions that are transformed, expanded or burnt up as they travel on.

We find clouds useful as a way of thinking about digital systems and their relation to the world. Clouds don't stack rigidly. Indeed we feel that Benjamin Bratton, and the overuse of his work, has burned the stack out, at least as a useful way of thinking further about relations; the stack is the stack is the stack – the inquiry, and the order, and the answer. Clouds have a different potential.

Our writing is centred on processes through which digital mediation has become and/or is becoming a pervasive condition of aspects of contemporary life; so that we're centrally concerned with how we live in the information cloud – and in the shadows it casts. But we also look outwards. We travel ourselves. We can't began and end with information, we can't stay hidden in the information cloud, or rely on a form of informational autarky. This is what technological determination provides, mistaking a kind of sectoral purchase for a universalizable outcome,

EXPANDED INTERSECTIONALITY AS A MODUS OPERANDI

So, we live in clouds and in the shadow of clouds. We respond to the complexity of cloud formations by exploring an expanded mode of intersectionality (an intra-sectionality); a project that requires recognition, and engagement at multiple scales, with heterogeneous intersections crossing within and between cloud formations of all kinds.

The intersections that order social engagement scale in, up, out and across. The giant cloud formations of capitalism, environmental systems and information, internally intersectional themselves, intersect. They have an intersectional relation. These intersections include those between gender, race, class and sexuality, and these constitute key conditions of our social becoming/situation. They generate demands for an intersectional politics, including one of recognition. They interoperate. These intersections and interoperations, their conditions of possibility and their enactment, constitute, if not a comprehensible totality (they definitely don't), then a system of a kind. This moreover, is a system that implicates 'us' (us humans in this case), even as 'we' don't entirely control it. It's an imbroglio, stupid – or perhaps it's just weather.

You don't need a weatherman to know which way the wind blows. Better – perhaps – be a semi-illegible woman-hood writing collective who/which already recognizes intersectionality as a condition of everyday life and so is clearer about how it might also be a principle operating at new scales . . .

WE RESPOND TO THE WEATHER
WITH TECHNOPHILE WRITING . . .

Our writing is technophile in that we want, in principle, not more (nor less) technology. We want different outcomes from the technologies with which we are transforming our own condition and our world today, and we want to forge different kinds of engagement with future technologies, or with thinking the future through technologies. We are technophiles in that our intervention into what needs to be done, our techno-politics, is not based on any principled adherence to primitivism, refusal or curtailment – neither as principles to be adopted in relation to technological trajectories in general, nor for thinking about technology for justice. We think blunt measures such as, 'more' or 'less' suck, mostly – more for whom? Less for whom?

... WITH WRITING THAT IS INTENDED AS AN INTERVENTION INTO OTHER TECHNOPHILE CRITIQUES OF THE GIVEN

Our writing links to (and draws on) other lines of more or less technophile inquiry that are also critical of accepting the inevitability of technology as given by markets. We engage particularly with those arguments that take as a central concern, questions of social justice, freedom, and equality, and which ask how to explore them afresh in the contexts of environmental limits. However, to recognize common ground and to respect fellow travellers is not to agree with the routes they take, nor to share their sense of where their designated routes might take all of us in the end. We have problems with some of these approaches, problems that are both deontological and consequentialist. In particular, we think there are problems with forms of critical techno-futurism and digital analysis that are very influential right now, if not quite hegemonic, in academic, and other committed writing, about computational culture. We think these are problems feminist approaches can begin to find ways to identify and address.

Is it a bit late in the day (and book) to set out the above? It might be, but these general positions just mesh with what we've been arguing for more obliquely in the first four chapters. Up to now we have been performing a critique and exploring what emerges through that performance, rather than setting out 'what we know' or making a straightforward case. In this final chapter, still rather un-enamoured with the straightforward, since it's such a bad way to map the world, we're going to change our tone (our mode of address), and we're going to move things along. Here is how:

One: we're going to review our own previous performances; what were we trying, not only to say, but to do, in our writing – or in writing as we did? That might entail questioning ourselves as authors, intellectuals, women, as an individual and as a collective. It seems to us that asking about the 'who' in writing is a particularly germane question in an era in which 'the individual' is a category at once most valourized (you who choose, you who are acted upon), and also (through dividuation and finely sliced categorization) most deleted.

We are going to assess where this writing performance has taken us so far, how we might travel on, and where we want to go. Our intention in these writing performances was to use various strategies – style, fiction, play, refusal, incredulity, expertise, sarcasm, authorial ambiguity, amongst them – to find a place that gives onto 'the digital' differently. This is not a place above the clouds, but is one that provides a different kind of perspective, and might help us make new demands or generate a different informational politics.

The place we have been driving towards, or trying to catch a glimpse of at least, has been envisaged as one we can feel at once at home *in*, but also estranged *from*. What is the point in journeying towards, if we simply circle back and land at the same old place, re-inventing the same old politics, the same old cheap compensations, and cruel divisions, but just with smarter technologies? We certainly don't wish to set out, travel, land and re-impose old social relations in a re-wallpapered prison, as if we had never really left; that would be collusion.

Two: We are going to make demands. We are going to produce a proposition (or 22), or at least lay out some theses. And if our propositions are rhetorical, our theses will be analytic and suggestive, programmatic and ad hoc. We want to insist both that the very grand stories and the very small ones intersect – and that their knowledge claims can both be taken seriously. The question of *how* the apparently incommensurable can be intersected, or interoperated, of how to turn what is analytic into what is programmatic, really matters. Haraway's sense that the storying of story matters, matters to us. For us, the point of travelling, of writing (where writing is seen in part as a narrative that opens a path, but not only as a narrative), is to demand and to adopt technologies for change. This suddenly sounds instrumental, perhaps (building not thinking). Our point, in putting it this way, is that calls for technologies for change cannot be equated with calls for changes in technology; the former reach far beyond the latter.

Our demands, or our theses, set out ways in which we could live in or with the clouds better. Proximately, this is a matter of responding to information's possibilities, as well as critiquing what it may do/what has been done with it. It is also a matter of assessment, intervention, critique and imagination. It is thus a matter of intervening beyond the present, in relation to the analysis of what has gone before and in relation to the possibilities for various futures. If we have our head in the clouds, that's both to look at what is there (a moment of analysis), and to inform our visions of what may become (the moment of utopian imagination). We want to disentangle what is made from what could be made and perhaps from what we think should be made. As part of that, we also ask what might be materialized beyond the usual limits of our imaginations, how we might best break out of the currently constraining horizon in new ways. The way might be to let the sparks rise higher, or raise a different wind:

> If she comes, said Le Guin's Ged, of the dragon human burnt girl child who found a way to fly, she will come from there out there on the horizon. If she does not come, she is there, dancing in the other wind . . .

Winds, clouds, shadows (and sparks) are germane here because, as we've already said, this final chapter moves between scales and levels and layers and their intersections; a techno-social and earthed ecology. This is the new weather, intrinsically technological, complexly connected, full of hard places that might be rocks, of rocks and hard places that may be opportunities, and of pathways that might be abandoned for climbing, scrambling, or refusing eithers and ors. It is in this space that we travel.

A PERFORMANCE REVIEW

Review, assess, demand; does this sound like a set of KPIs? If so, we're sorry. It's not the kind of performance review that demands credible 'evidence', where credibility claims are rooted in solutionist illusions, that we're interested in. The key to this review is what we've written and how we've written it.

Here let's go back to clouds and stacks and weather and to the status of models and metaphors in our current formation, and what they can/cannot address.

For us, the urgent/intractable problem, simultaneously posited and set aside because deemed solved in stack approaches, is not that things relate, but how relations operate. In the case of the stack, much that goes under the same name (how machine ontologies relate to ontological questions concerning human beings, for instance) may be 'stack-systemically' divided into operations undertaken in multiple layers. This can be useful, but it can also and often and too easily, suggest isomorphic and terminal connections between processes divided vertically when the reality of the intersections is that they are multi-directional, complex, partial and provisional. Possibilities for thinking about relations in process may be precisely what is rendered illegible in the layered divisions of stacked relations. Stacked relations depend on the self-identity of things that are stacked.

Despite their computational associations, stack principles are not new, of course. Some famous old stacks that were developed in order to put things in their proper place, indeed to enlighten us, spring to mind. Think of those great vertical chains of being: animal, human, angel and up. And of Pope who wrote of them, in Alexandrine couplets, with an elegance belying his own sense of incipient chaos and the universal darkness coming to cover us all.

The stack might be a tempting model partly because it is temptingly tidy and contains the seeds of its own completion. We're untidy. We think the problem is how to take notice of these relationships; as these are promised (powerfully, performatively), and as they operate productively, and how to do so without succumbing to ambitions to understand them completely, comprehensively, or neatly.

So let's fight the stack and its normative orderings of the who and how and the 'through which', and those inevitable stages of chained operations through which, across which, all things pass. We'd rather think about combined and uneven development, with its leaps and bounds – and its recognition of the paradoxical lethargy at the heart of domination. We prefer the cloudiness of clouds to the stacked up stack, or the chained up chain; all that being and doing in the right order, horizontal and vertical. The stack is not a found model (the real shape of things). It just pretends to be. There need to be better figures/models to capture the state of affairs, right now and also as a guide to politics.

A different kind of re-ordering is needed. We've pushed for a different way of critiquing/thinking/responding to information and mediation. This book has been getting at that problem in myriad ways for a hundred pages now. We have said: 'drive a car through the stack'. We have forced into relation the claims for the radically ambitious and the socially conservative, violating stack layers. We have refused the division between one kind of genetic mediation and other kinds of healthcare. We have demanded/performed different forms of care for, and different ideas of caring for, technology.

All these things we have done to respond to a set of very practical questions/problematics. How to rethink the way technologies (that are pervasive) can be understood/used by/developed by humans (in their worlds which are also technological), in ways that are not those that are thought now, in ways that are not now put into operation. Why don't we want those ways? Because they don't produce freedom; they don't take us beyond old inequalities and identifications, and they don't capture the ways in which we need to live in the shadow with global reach – the Anthropocene and more.

We ourselves . . .

Our stack attack begins with a refusal. We are refusing a key term at the heart of the given relation between ourselves and information, or between ourselves and the model. We attack the isolation of the self, the 'who' to be worked upon, the self who gets to choose, or be nudged, the personalized/dividuated/sovereign self. The point is, we are set up in all of these ways; this is how we are valourized by digital information. This is the self who may act, and who may choose, but who always sees back from the cloud what the cloud chooses to give back – which is an image of the self. A very particular kind of cloud formation is responsible for the beautiful illusion/refraction phenomena of the Brockengespenst image. This happens when the light behind a climber projects their image onto the clouds, producing a giant self, the shadow of a self in the clouds. Experiencing this effect you become a god to yourself, or a dancing shadow, but either way, you are visible only to yourself, the image is in your own eye. To experience this weather, to be subject to the cloud that reflects/refracts/expands and atomizes the self, even in the company of other walkers, might give pause. It is invoked as a parable here. We live in the shadow of many clouds, and need to ask about our relations to our own and others' shadows and bodies, about the flesh and bones and technologies and materials and the symbolic structures of the social order. We need to ask how this self relates to the environment in which we find ourselves, which we have co-constituted. This is to say that we are ordered through computational systems, a techno-cultural order that is at once symbolic and imaginary, as well as real. This order can be responded to; you cannot stop the Brockengespenst but you can turn away from the mountain view. We wish to refuse the physics and optics of the Brockengespenst image, with its dividuated bigging up, as a way of understanding the contemporary informational order and the kinds of social subjects it can produce. When we say refuse, we mean cheat.

This book is written by three people who declare themselves a non-I- and who would also wish to question the conventional sum that gives 'we' 'simply as 'I' plus. I plus I plus I = we. Writing as us and as we, as our selves and as a 'one' that is not one, has a number of consequences. It has produced an unevenness in tone, and a set of contradictions; for whom was the shadow of the cloud found on the lung of their own mother, and who agreed to share this experience?

Am I or she, or all of us, writing this now? Writing as selves, and as a group, has let us think through some problems in somewhat different ways. Writing together we are neither ourselves, nor a fully subsumed collective, nor yet do we wish to be a singular we, a new 'I' that is forged out of a collective, compressed back down. So what are we? What kind of giant could come back to this 'us' out of the clouds, if we found out how to see it, and forced it to see us, as now possessed of a kind of com- binatory power.

Monstrous ontologies and all: and the renewed 'promise of monsters'

We, writing together, can be something more combinatory than additive. This suggests the grounds of a different way of thinking. It might let us slip out for a bit (out of the personalized world valourized by the platforms, and the solipsistic narcissistic self-interest they actively cultivate). Writing together gets us out of the confinement that emerges when there is only self/other, individual sovereign or collective (as the additive joining/binding together of those individuals), to choose from. If our writing isn't authored like that, if we reject that binary, what does that do? What does that make us? We find here the beginnings of a figure for a new form of solidarity.

We are Author

If we are a monstrous being, we are also a monstrous author, and we are definitely up for being that. We see no reason to refuse the role of the author, stolen back over and over again by writers who recognized the death of every author but themselves from the mid-twentieth century on. We want to be author, but to expand the term, break it, use it against its historical desire to define itself.

Our sense is of a common authorship, an authorship entailing writing selves joined and distributed, contradictory, but also consistent. We are clear that we write from and in feminism. Shared qualities across our component selves constitute boundaries (permeable, and not so permeable) and map out our common author-identity, our identity in common, and our non-innocent situatedness. Our intention was never to use this kind of authorship to hide, for instance to occlude our gendered or raced identity, our generation, class or location. This kind of anonymity too easily produces claims to false universality, and/or seeks to avoid the need to check its privilege (our privilege). Our hope is that this kind of authorship enables the kind of writing identity that can, recognizing responsibility, and requiring situatedness as an ethics of writing, nonetheless find a way not to get caught. We might, that is, be able to write/navigate/do things in ways that we couldn't as feminist authors on our own.

It is useful to assert and refuse authorship. And it is intriguing to find oneself in a body of writing that is over 150 years old . . .

Unheroics

Writing jointly informs the kinds of protagonist we wish to be. This might be a matter of heroics. Hannah Arendt said (perhaps partly disparagingly) that heroes have and do things with stories. Partly what they do is dash around and complete them and close them down. In this sense, the violence of the ending is narratologically understandable in terms of the terminal identity of the identifiable protagonist and their actions. A conception of earth as a landscape for heroes/heroics seems to us utterly inadequate or not apt for thinking about our future right now. The dragons are dead. The heroic story divides the hero or the protagonist – and their possibility for action – from the rest of us. Consider Odysseus' elite mode of heroic travelling (me, me, me), both egotistical (and ineffective); he faced the sirens by getting himself staked to a mast and plugging the ears of his crew so he alone could hear while they sailed. Well, we're not to be bound, we don't think anybody else should be rendered insensible either, certainly not if they're the ones doing much of the work. The need is for more navigators and more witnesses, for a new fabric of understanding and writing.

We wonder what that sailor thought, his ears bound, but his hearing eyes open, understanding, not what the sirens sang, but what they signed ...

Because we are particular kind of author, we refuse a particular kind of protagonism.

Bodies and their edges

Since we are multiple and also in common, we question our boundaries. Our common body can assist in exploding the tediously instantiated demand to terminally cleave between human and other, nature and world. Mediation as a pervasive fact of today's life makes clear how this cleavage was always a fiction. We were all already, as mediated beings, multiple, not reducible to singular ones. It is partly because we recognize this – in theory, in our theorizing of the possibilities of information, that we have formed ourself as this collective-which-is-not one.

We need Solidarity beyond the Additive Collective.

WE ARE GOING TO MAKE DEMANDS/THESES

It is good to take on the Ambiguous Utopia of Combinatory Woman.

21 propositions

1. Voice: Too much academic writing on computation valourizes sovereign scholars and particular citation practices. Against this, computational cultures aggregate data and delete the author. We assert the need for new forms of scholarly writing in response. Voice can be collective and plural, not universal. Voice can be collective but specific: white, female, academic, queer, for instance. Voice can be some kind of we/us/I with purchase in alliance with others. The corollary of writing differently is also listening in a new way. We would like to redefine 'you' too – but we're not sure that's our job.
2. Collectivity: Data dividuates, and in doing so, exacerbates tendencies towards extreme individualism and a mode of personal solutionism that presumes technology might fix us. There can't be a response to computational cultures, as extensions of neoliberalism that remains individual. New forms of collectivity and solidarity need to be explored.

3. Narrative: Technological futurists have big new stories to tell – while in response, accelerationism and the new materialism abhor narrative and representation in their search for a better future. We're not giving up stories. On the contrary, it is necessary to re-story stories about technology. We want to intervene in the storying: there is a need for new accounts about what is extant, but badly told. The point is to break boundaries that constrain our imaginations within the horizon of the present by creating new fictional worlds.

4. Making theory in the world: Theory cannot stand on its own. Technology can't be left to the technologists. The peril is to mistake making for interventionism and to mistake scale operations as effective intervention at all scales. The old binary of technology and use needs to be discarded. Critical intervention needs to rethink its point of engagement: not at the end, but all the way through.

5. Criticality: Technology insists on its own given-ness. Against that, we need to rethink and reassert the value of criticality. That's the only way to act rather than react, and to find a way to contest the presentism and destining of the technological future. The alternatives to criticality in academia are in the end collusions. To give up critique in relation to computational culture is to give up the world. We claim critical theory is generative, is interventionist, is world-making, deals in the material: the material, the symbolic, the coded, the embodied, the post-bodied. It is not the other of any of these, but their beginning.

6. Abstraction is delusion: The rehashing of Futurist delusions that pure technology produced pure light, pure principle, pure force, for instance in later versions of accelerationism, that are fundamentally decent, arise out of a process through which technology is stripped of all but 'machine'. No process, no human, no context, no history. No politics. The point for feminist technophile politics is that such abstraction is a delusion. Acknowledging this is a way to reconcile flesh and machines in a (re)newed feminist politics.

7. Scale: Technology gives us new scales. There's an ethics of the scalable, which needs to inform how we judge and read the knowledge we find at scales. Scale is not size, nor a big/small binary, but a new range of possibilities. To prefer scaleability over size isn't simply to demand more places to see – from the god's eye to the quark. The point is to make decisions about which scales to employ and when. This involves judgement. Who may see and at what scale? What

scales? Both of these are more important than defining the 'right 'scale at which to live, or know, or learn.

8. Limits: A computational feminism without awareness of ecological limits makes no sense. That's not new. At issue is how to take limits seriously, and how to refuse the apparent escapes offered by the technological; open sky, informational plentitude as light and air, calculations costing the cloud that consistently underplays its material load in favour of the algorithmic benefit. To believe it is possible to move into a new world without being poisoned by the old is as irresponsible as giving in to the apocalypse. Feminism has a tradition of challenging given limits – bodily essentialisms for instance – while remaining aware of finitude. We should use this approach to re-examine environmental limits; not to become deniers, but to inaugurate change.

9. Feminist epistemology: Feminist engagements with automation and new forms of intelligence provoke/demand new forms of engagement with knowledge and the limits of knowledge. Against paranoid desires to know all through technology – which find their correspondence in fears that technology knows all – we propose to celebrate/generate new forms of human machine engagement that produce a different balance. It is not possible to open all black boxes nor can we relinquish responsibility for what's inside. This tension constitutes a new episteme of the knowable and unknowable. The task for feminism in these new contexts remains a matter of making a cut. Thinking about new relations of automation, knowledge and power doesn't mean making a division: the human on one side and the machine on the other. On the contrary, a feminist politics asks how the cut is made, and who and which groups are being allowed to make it. Old stories about whose knowledge counts still need to be contested in new conditions of knowledge making.

10. We do not cede utopia to the technocrats.

11. Modelling: We don't give away modelling either. You can't have a model of social justice if you don't have a model of the social. You can't have a sense of the engagement between technology, culture and environment unless you model that too. However, we don't want the models we've got, the technical, the pure the abstract. There is a need to think systematically about what models do and what they elide. We need planning, models, systems that are not abstract or totalizing – correlationism isn't enough – the data doesn't speak for

itself. New models need at once to avoid the arid closures of protocol generalized, and the fiction that models may capture the whole. We are seeking impure models that reintroduce history in objects and objects into histories in new ways, and recognise the complexity and excess of any system.

12. Radical intersubjectivity: Intersectional politics recognizes social division, inequality and multiple forms of subjectivity. Radical intersectionality insists on rethinking the grounds across which the intersectional occurs as environmental and technological. A feminist politics for the digital isn't just about mapping across old intersections into new milieu, but rather about how these relations are reconstituted through technology and how technology itself becomes an actor in their operation. How can algorithms that categorize race become tools for liberation rather than the means of exacerbating exploitation, for example?

13. Temporality: Techno-stories tend to start at the beginning or the end: origins, end points, upgrades. Computational technology is obsessed with its own present and newest version. Now is always good, the future will always be better. This leaves the past as only a stepping stone to what came about anyway: a lethally self-justifying origin story that doesn't count its own costs. It's more interesting to start somewhere else and it matters because these stories hide the cost of the past in the conspicuous successes of the marketized present and the future that is promised. Let's avoid ends and beginnings.

14. Writing: Writing is powerful. It does things in the world. It acts. Critical writing can intervene in the making of things and worlds, that are too often viewed as objects in themselves, systems outside of representation or language. Doing things with words – as a naming act, a claiming, a dividing, a joining – has material effects. Words inaugurate. Technology is not born; it is made. And so are we. Words are ways to break with the smooth surface of the technological given. Deconstruction never only happened in the text, and writing is the principle mechanism of deconstruction. It is a technology and a strategy for initiating change. It is this aspect of its force and power that feminists, amongst others, have long recognized and deployed. This is one basis for rebuilding a politics at a time when power tends to be invested in code's performativity not language's inaugural capacity.

15. Bodies and minds: We defend the need for recognizing and acknowledging multiple forms of intelligence and mind; including embodied intelligence, emotional reason. But we also refuse any division between emotion and the body on the one hand, and reason on the other. We don't make a fetish of the body as female/feminine, but rather seek a different understanding of mind/body relations. And we categorically refuse to retain emotion for ourselves and give away reason to the other side. A feminism ambitious for technology and for itself seeks on the one hand to break any essentialized sense of what bodies should be, or what minds should be, and on the other to engage with and celebrate the possibilities for new kinds of augmentation.

16. SMART: Feminism is smart. We draw on our history in order to respond to claims that smart is the future, is progress, speed, abstraction or simply a value added dimension to consumer products. Analytic, tactical, radically intersectional feminism sees smart differently, claims it differently. Bringing other forms of intelligence not often valourized, recognized or legitimated to the table, opens the way for far more diverse and exciting ways to rethink how computational technologies can remake us.

17. The post-digital isn't: We are not post-digital. On the contrary, we need to recognize the centrality of the digital. The work of contestation isn't undertaken by declaring that what has become infrastructural is no longer of interest.

18. Modulation and social control: Predictive algorithms increase the scale and scope of forms of behaviour modification. Social subjects increasingly are not invited to take decisions, but are nudged towards socially acceptable actions and practices. This form of social control – representing a new form of modulation as social discipline – revives behaviourism as an efficient form of governance, while forgetting its active demand that humans forgo freedom. The feminism we want cares about liberation.

19. Generation: Computational technology is in love with the new, and pretends to exist only in the present. Feminism shouldn't fall for this. To fall in with the claim that new is always better and that we need to replace the old, would be to forget that technology itself embeds, that older technologies continue to enact, even while attention has shifted to the new. We contest the idea of generation itself, as a way of understanding humans and their relations with technol-

ogy. Generation as a social category is ideologically conservative, and misreads the relationship between flesh bodies and social and technological possibilities. The simultaneity and overlapping contingencies of experience are not adequately defined through a notion of generation, or through the way that this is currently mapped. The organization of the life course is profoundly intersected with the technological conditions in which we find ourselves: feminism should not work with categories of age and experience as givens, and as a given sequence or succession, but rather use technology to revolutionize these and all categories of subjection/subjectification.

20. Informational politics: A feminist informational politics declares the grounds it contests to be as broad as the spread of information itself. This includes communication circuits, but also the myriad other forms in which information comes to govern us; from everyday sexism (as hashtag activism for instance), to everyday computational discrimination exercised via social algorithms, to data issues in health, migration and ecology. The challenge is not only to recognize an expanded zone of activities here, but also to consider their temporal extension. Our interventions matter beyond the immediate moment. The point is not to be a symptom of the informational, but to mobilize with it. We recognize the tension here between staying with the problem and becoming trapped in the present.

21. Insurgent feminism: We define insurgent feminism as writerly, radically intersectional, agonistic, angry, imaginative and ambitious. A feminist insurgence is predicated on not forgetting where it has come from and on not needing to know exactly where it is going. We need to do much more than seek to manage risk and predict the technological future, which is the future of our environment.

The point is to break open what has become a closed set of demands and desires. No more leaning in. Break out! We want more, and better contested, future imaginings, at new scales. Thinking again, with urgency, for better ways of living together in and with the world. We need to act collectively beyond the solipsistic self-serving fatalism of the everyday and the Anthropocenic 'we're fucked'. Which in any case translates into a technological politics of quietism and acceptance of the status quo. We need to think again about how to think and act through technology.

Bibliography

Adams, C. (1990) *The Sexual Politics of Meat: A Feminist Vegetarian Ethic*. London: Bloomsbury.

Arendt, H. (1958) *The Human Condition*. Chicago: University of Chicago Press.

Barad, K. (2000) 'Reconceiving Scientific Literacy as Agential Literacy. Or, Learning How to Intra-act Responsibly with the World', in R. Reid and S. Traweek (eds) *Doing Science + Culture. How Cultural and Interdisciplinary Studies are Changing the Way We Look at Science and Medicine*. New York and London: Routledge, pp. 221–59.

Barad, K. (2007) *Meeting the Universe Halfway: Quantum Physics and the Entanglement of Matter and Meaning*. Durham, NC: Duke University Press.

Bassett, C. (1999) 'A manifesto against manifestos', *Next Cyberfeminist International*, 8–13 March 1999, Rotterdam.

Bassett, C. (2004) *The Arc and the Machine*. Manchester: Manchester University Press.

Bassett, C. (2010) 'Impossible, Admirable, Androgyne: Firestone, Technology, and Utopia', in M. Merck and S. Sandford (eds) *Further adventures of the dialectic of sex*. London: Palgrave.

Bassett, C. (2013) 'Feminism, Expertise and the Computational Turn', in H. Thornham and E. Weissmann (eds) *Renewing Feminism: Narratives, Fantasies and Futures*. London: IB Tauris, pp. 199–214.

Berlant, L. (2011) *Cruel Optimism*. Durham, NC: Duke University Press.

Bird Rose, D. and Robin, L. (2004) 'The Ecological Humanities in Action: An Invitation', *Australian Humanities Review*. http://australianhumanitiesreview.org/2004/04/01/the-ecological-humanities-in-action-an-invitation/.

Brown, P.G. and Timmerman, P. (2015) (eds) *Ecological Economics for the Anthropocene*, New York: Columbia University Press.

Bryson, M. and Stacey, J. (2013) 'Cancer Knowledge in the Plural: Queering the Biopolitics of Narrative and Affective Mobilities', *Journal of Medical Humanities* 34(2): 197–212.

Bould M. and Miéville, C. (2009) *Red Planets: Marxism and Science Fiction*. London: Pluto Press.

Carson, R. (1962) *Silent Spring*. London: Penguin.

Chertoff, E. (2012) 'Eulogy for a Sex Radical: Shulamith Firestone's Forgotten Feminism', *The Atlantic*. http://thefuturelaboratory.com/uk/.

Cixous, H. (1976) 'The Laugh of the Medusa', translated by Keith Cohen and Paula Cohen, *Signs*, 1: 4. Summer, pp. 875–93.

Cixous, H. and Clément, C. (2008) [1975] *The Newly Born Woman*, translated by Betsy Wing. London and Minneapolis: University of Minnesota Press.

Cockburn, C. (1992) 'The Circuit of Technology: Gender, identity and Power', Hirsch and Silverstone (eds) *Consuming Technologies, Media and Information in Domestic Spaces*. London: Routledge, pp. 32–48.

Cohen, T. and Colebrook, C. (2016) 'Preface', in T. Cohen, C. Colebrook and J. Hillis Miller, *Twilight of the Anthropocene Idols*. London: Open Humanities Press, pp. 7–20.

Cowen, D. (2010) 'Containing Insecurity: Logistic Space, U.S. Port Cities, and the 'War on Terror', in S. Graham (ed) *Disrupted Cities. When Infrastructure Fails*. New York and London: Routledge, pp. 69–85.

Crenshaw, K. 'Mapping the Margins: Intersectionality, Identity Politics, and Violence against Women of Color', *Stanford Law Review*, 43(6): 1241–99.

Davis, A.Y. (1981) *Women, Race and Class*. New York: Vintage Books.

Davis, N. and David, R. (2016) 'Tech House of the Future: Take a Look Around', *Guardian*, 4 December 2016.

De Lauretis, T. (1984) *Alice Doesn't: Feminism, Semiotics, Cinema*. Bloomington: Indiana University Press.

Federici, S. (2012) *Revolution at Point Zero: Housework, Reproduction, and Feminist Struggle*. Oakland: PM Press.

Franklin, S. (2000) 'Life Itself: Global Nature and the Genetic Imaginary', in S. Franklin, C. Lury and J. Stacey (eds), *Global Nature, Global Culture*. London: Sage, pp. 188–227.

Gabrys, J. (2011) *Rubbish: A Natural History of Electronics*. Ann Arbor: University of Michigan Press.

Gauthier, X. (1985) 'Why Witches?' in E. Marks and I. de Courtivron (eds) *New French Feminisms*. Sussex: The Harvester Press, pp. 199–203.

Graham, S. (2010) (ed) *Disrupted Cities. When Infrastructure Fails*. New York and London: Routledge.

Gray, M. and Suri, S. (2019) *Ghost Work: How to Stop Silicon Valley from Building a New Global Underclass*. Houghton Mifflin Harcourt.

Gregg, M. (2011) *Work's Intimacy*. Cambridge, UK: Polity Press.

Gregg, M. (2015) 'Inside the Data Spectacle', *Television and New Media*, 16(1) 37–51.

Haran, J. (2018) *Genetic Fictions: Genes, Gender and Genre*. Cardiff: University of Wales Press.

Haraway, Donna J. (2012) *SF: Speculative Fabulation and String Figures*. dOCUMENTA (13) Ostfildern: Hatje Cantz Verlag.

Haraway, Donna J. (2016) *Staying with the Trouble. Making Kin in the Chthulucene*. Durham and London: Duke University Press.

Hayles, K.N. (2005) *My Mother Was a Computer: Digital Subjects and Literary Texts*. Chicago: University of Chicago Press.

International Labour Organization (2015). *Women and the Future of Work, Beijing +20 and Beyond*. www.ilo.org/wcmsp5/groups/public/---dgreports/---dcomm/documents/briefingnote/wcms_348087.pdf.

Janda, R. and Lehun, R. (2015) 'Justice Claims Underpinning Ecological Economics', in P.G. Brown and P. Timmerman (eds) *Ecological Economics for the Anthropocene*. New York: Columbia University Press, pp. 89–119.

Jarrett, K. (2015) *Feminism, Labour and Digital Media: The Digital Housewife*. London: Routledge.

Jürgenssen, B. (1974–5) 'Apron', Photographic work.

Feminist Avant-Garde of the 1970s: Works from the Verbund Collection. https://thephotographersgallery.org.uk/whats-on/past-exhibitions/feminist-avant-garde.

Kaye, L. (2000) *Who Wrote the Book of Life? A History of the Genetic Code*. Stanford: Stanford University Press.

Keller, E. (2000) *The Century of the Gene*. Cambridge, US: Harvard University Press.

Kember, S. (2003) *Cyberfeminism and Artificial Life*. London: Routledge.

Kember, S. (2016) *iMedia: The Gendering of Objects, Environments and Smart Materials*. London: Palgrave Macmillan.

Kember, S. and Zylinska, J. (2012) *Life After New Media. Mediation as a Vital Process*. Cambridge, US: MIT Press.

Kerr, A. (2005) 'Understanding genetic disease in a socio-historical context: a case study of cystic fibrosis', *Sociology of Health and Illness*, 27.7 (2005), 873–96.

King, K. (2013) *Networked Reenactments: Stories Transdisciplinary Knowledges Tell*. Durham, NC: Duke University Press.

Klein, M. (1984). *Envy and Gratitude and Other Works 1946–1963*. London: The Hogarth Press.

Latour, B. (2013) translated by Catherine Porter, *An Inquiry into Modes of Existence. An Anthropology of the Moderns*. Cambridge, US: Harvard University Press.

Lee, S. (2014) 'Empowerment in personal Genetics, Gibbon', S. Joseph, G. Mozersky, J. zur Neiden, and S. Palfner (2014) *Breast Cancer Gene Research and Medical Practices*. London: Routledge.

Lorde, A. (1980) *Age, Race, Class, and Sex; Women Redefining Difference'*.

Lorde, A. 1984 [2007] 'The Master's Tools Will Never Dismantle the Master's House', *Sister Outsider: Essays and Speeches*, pp. 110–14. Berkeley, CA: Crossing Press.

Lorde, A. (1984) 'Age, Race, Class and Sex: Women Defining Difference', *Sister Outsider: Essays and Speeches*. Berkeley, CA: Crossing Press, pp. 114–23.

Malik, S. (2006) 'Information and Knowledge', M. Fraser, S. Kember, C. Lury (eds) *Inventive Life Approaches to the New Vitalism*. London: Sage Publishing.

McNeil, M. (1987) 'Introduction', in *Gender and Expertise*. London: Free Association Press, pp. 1–9.

McNeil, M. (2007) *Feminist Cultural Studies of Science and Technology*. London: Routledge.

McRobbie, A. (2009) *The Aftermath of Feminism: Gender, Culture and Social Change*. London: Sage.

Moore, J.W. (2016) (ed) *Anthropocene or Capitalocene? Nature, History, and the Crisis of Capitalism*. Oakland: Kairos/PM Press.

Mouffe, C. (2005) *On the Political*. London and New York: Routledge.

Negri, T. and Hardt, M. (2012) 'Declaration', *Critical Legal Thinking*. http://criticallegalthinking.com/2012/06/14/declaration-hardt-negri/.

Odzeki, R. (2014) *A Tale for the Time Being*. New York: Viking Press.

O'Riordan, K. (2010) *The Genome Incorporated*. London: Routledge.

O'Riordan, K. (2011) 'Writing Biodigital Life: Personal Genomes and Digital Media', *Biography*, 34(1).

Raworth, K. (2014) 'Must the Anthropocene be a Manthropocene?' *Guardian*, 20 October 2014. www.theguardian.com/commentisfree/2014/oct/20/anthropocene-working-group-science-gender-bias.

Reardon, J. (2004) *Race to the Finish: Identity and Governance in an Age of Genomics*. Princeton: Princeton University Press.

Reardon, J. (2017) *The Postgenomic Condition: Ethics, Justice, Knowledge After the Genome*. Chicago: Chicago University Press.

Roof, J. (2007) *The Poetics of DNA*. Minneapolis: University of Minnesota Press.

Scott, J. (1991) 'The Evidence of Experience', *Critical Inquiry*, 17(4): 773–97.

Stabile, C. (1994) *Feminism and the Technological Fix*. Manchester: Manchester University Press.

Syms, M. (2018) 'The Mundane Afrofuturist Manifesto', http://martinesyms.com/the-mundane-afrofuturist-manifesto/ (accessed 04/06/2018).

Terranova, T. (2014) 'Red Stack Attack! Algorithms, Capital and the Automation of the Common', R. Mackay and A. Avanessian (eds) *#Accelerate# the accelerationist reader*. London: Urbanomic.

Thomas, S. (2013) *Technobiophilia: Nature and Cyberspace*. London: Bloomsbury.

Thompson, A.C. (2016) 'What are the ingredients to the smart kitchen?" www.cnet.com/news/what-are-the-ingredients-to-the-smart-kitchen (accessed 01/07/2019).

Van Djick, J. (1998) *Imagenation: Popular Images of Genetics*. New York: New York University Press.

Wark, M. (2015) *Molecular Red. Theory for the Anthropocene*. London and New York: Verso.

Wertheim, M. (2000) *The Pearly Gates of Cyberspace: A History of Space from Dante to the Internet*, W. V. Norton.

Whyte, K.P. (2018) 'Indigenous Science (Fiction) for the Anthropocene: Ancestral Dystopias and Fantasies of the Climate Change Crisis', https://michiganstate.academia.edu/KyleWhyte (accessed 04/06/2018).

Index

The Pluto Press Newsletter

Hello friend of Pluto!

Want to stay on top of the best radical books
we publish?

Then sign up to be the first to hear about our
new books, as well as special events,
podcasts and videos.

You'll also get 50% off your first order with us
when you sign up.

Come and join us!

Go to bit.ly/PlutoNewsletter

Made in United States
Orlando, FL
18 June 2022

18920112R00082